TANKS
OF WORLD WARS I AND II

TANKS
OF WORLD WARS I AND II

- An illustrated A–Z catalogue of tanks, armoured vehicles, tank destroyers, command versions and specialized tanks from 1916–45

- From the prototype No. 1 Lincoln Machine "Little Willie" to the Panzers and D-Day Funnies

- Includes over 275 colour and black-and-white archive photographs

George Forty

southwater

This edition is published by Southwater, an imprint of Anness Publishing Ltd, Hermes House, 88–89 Blackfriars Road, London SE1 8HA; tel. 020 7401 2077; fax 020 7633 9499

www.southwaterbooks.com; www.annesspublishing.com

Anness Publishing has a picture agency outlet for images for publishing, promotions or advertising. Please visit our website www.practicalpictures.com for more information.

UK agent: The Manning Partnership Ltd; tel. 01225 478444; fax 01225 478440; sales@manning-partnership.co.uk

UK distributor: Grantham Book Services Ltd; tel. 01476 541080; fax 01476 541061; orders@gbs.tbs-ltd.co.uk

North American agent/distributor: National Book Network; tel. 301 459 3366; fax 301 429 5746; www.nbnbooks.com

Australian agent/distributor: Pan Macmillan Australia; tel. 1300 135 113; fax 1300 135 103; customer.service@macmillan.com.au

New Zealand agent/distributor: David Bateman Ltd; tel. (09) 415 7664; fax (09) 415 8892

Publisher: Joanna Lorenz
Project Editor: Felicity Forster
Copy Editor and Indexer: Tim Ellerby

Cover Design: Balley Design Associates
Designer: Design Principals
Production Controller: Lee Sargent

ETHICAL TRADING POLICY

Because of our ongoing ecological investment programme, you, as our customer, can have the pleasure and reassurance of knowing that a tree is being cultivated on your behalf to naturally replace the materials used to make the book you are holding. For further information about this scheme, go to www.annesspublishing.com/trees

Previously published as part of a larger volume, *The World Encyclopedia of Tanks*

PAGE 1: **Mark V Light Tank.** PAGE 2: **A12 Infantry Tank Mark II Matilda II.** PAGE 3: **PzKpfw I Ausf B Light Tank (Command Version).**
BELOW: **Canadian-built Sherman Grizzly I Medium Tank.**

Contents

Introduction

What is a tank? Expressed in its simplest terms, a tank can be defined as a means of transporting firepower about on the battlefield, with its weapon system and crew protected from direct enemy fire. This revolutionary weapon has been in existence for under a hundred years, and in that time it has become one of the most important and indispensable components of the battle-winning All Arms Team. The tank is just one of the many types of Armoured Fighting Vehicle (AFV) found on the battlefield. What makes it special is the careful blend of its three basic characteristics – firepower, protection and mobility – into a lethal mix that can bring instantaneous, accurate, direct fire to bear, whenever and wherever it is needed, day and night, whether on the move or stationary. These three characteristics can be blended together in differing amounts to produce very different results, as can be seen in the directory section of this book.

Firepower is undoubtedly the most important characteristic because it is a tank's reason for being. The type and size of weapon system can vary enormously, and as this becomes larger and more sophisticated, the carrying vehicle invariably increases in both size and weight as there is more to protect.

If a tank is to achieve its mission, then an effective means of protection is vital. Although this can be achieved in a variety of ways, the basis is usually some form of armour plate. Continual improvements in the strength, quality and ease of

TOP: **Firepower. Even light tanks like these Polish 7TPs presented an awesome sight en masse. They initially proved to be a match for the German Blitzkrieg tanks, but were sadly too few to make a lasting impression.** ABOVE: **Protection. The commander of this PzKpfw IV Medium Tank clearly feels that he can rely on his armoured protection while closing in on a Russian strongpoint, as also do the accompanying infantry sheltering behind.**

production of armour were achieved during both World Wars, a major development, for example, being the use of cast armour rather than riveted plate. There are also other ways of providing protection, such as limiting size, lowering silhouette, camouflaging the tell-tale shape and using aids such as local smoke to help it "disappear". Inevitably as the tank's protection has become more and more sophisticated, so too have the

ABOVE: **The use of camouflage paint in irregular patterns was another means of protection, here assisting this Vickers light 6 Ton Tank to blend with its background.** RIGHT: **Mobility.** Some Italian Carro Veloce 33 Tankettes show off their tracked mobility by surmounting this sharp "knife-edge" obstacle.

anti-tank weapons ranged against it. Therefore its protection must be able to deal with all manner of attacks, from ground level – such as mines – through a vast range of hand-held/vehicle-borne guns and other missiles that can attack at any level, to specific top-attack weapons. To all of this must be added a tank's deadliest foe – another tank, with its weapon system firing more and more sophisticated ammunition specifically designed to penetrate armour.

Mobility is the third vital characteristic, and again as the tank became larger and heavier, increasingly more powerful powerplant, transmission and suspension were needed to move it over all types of terrain. Cross-country, the track clearly won over the wheel, and good mobility was essential if the tank was to achieve its varying missions. Weight affected its portability, especially by air or over water. Post-war tanks eventually reached their ultimate size and weight, so there is now a trend towards lighter, smaller, more portable tanks. However, this in turn puts the smaller tank at a distinct disadvantage in any tank versus tank engagements, when faced with a larger, better protected and better armed enemy, so tank development can be a vicious circle.

This book contains a wide selection of tanks that saw service in two World Wars. We have deliberately confined our coverage to the more important and interesting models worldwide, so while it is definitely not an exhaustive encyclopedia, it will give the reader a good indication of what the tank is all about.

The tank ended World War II in a pre-eminent position in the land battlefield and has lost none of its usefulness during the turbulent days that have followed. Time and time again tanks have shown themselves to be a potent force on the battlefield, not yet superseded as "Queen of the Battlefield" by any other weapon system. In the hands of well-trained, highly professional soldiers, the awesome power of the tank still lives on and will continue to do so into the foreseeable future. FEAR NAUGHT!

Key to flags

For the specification boxes, the national flag that was current at the time of the tank's use is shown.

Australia

Czechoslovakia

France

Germany: World War I

Germany: World War II

Hungary

Italy

Japan

Poland

Sweden

United Kingdom

USA

USSR

The History of Tanks

The history of the tank has very largely been the history of 20th-century ground warfare, this revolutionary new weapon being conceived to help break the early battlefield stalemate of World War I. Later it had mixed fortunes in the years of peace following 1918, but came back into its own during World War II and has maintained its pre-eminent position ever since. Tanks have been produced in all shapes and sizes throughout their history. Nevertheless, without exception, they have all had the basic characteristics of firepower, protection and mobility. It is how these are balanced together that makes a critical difference to their effectiveness. During the tank's history some of its original roles have been taken over by other types of Armoured Fighting Vehicle (AFV). Nevertheless, the ability of the tank to carry firepower about on the battlefield with a protected crew and weapons has remained essential. Having shown its potential in the later battles of World War I, the tank played a major role on both sides in many of the land battles of World War II, and can undoubtedly claim the lion's share of plaudits for the Allied victory on land.

LEFT: **At the heart of the success of the German Blitzkrieg tactics was the excellent PzKpfw IV Medium Tank, which, thanks to its far-sighted designers, remained the backbone of the *Panzerwaffe* throughout World War II.**

Evolution of the tank

Since earliest times humankind has searched for bigger and better weapons with which to defend themselves and destroy their enemies. Without doubt each one must have initially appeared to be invincible on the battlefield, more fearsome than its predecessor. None has been more effective than the tank, a revolutionary weapon system, tracing its ancestry back partly to the war chariot, partly to the armoured war elephant and partly to a mechanical war machine in the fertile mind of Leonardo da Vinci. Not until the 20th century was it possible to propel a suitably armoured vehicle containing a crew and its weapons across all types of terrain. The invention of the internal combustion engine, modern methods of fabricating armour plate and the caterpillar track all combined to make this possible.

The stimulus for this new weapon came about in 1914, following the stalemate on the Western Front after the First Battle of Ypres. Neither side could advance because the defences of the other were too strong. The artillery shell, machine-gun, barbed wire and never-ending trenches stretching from the Belgian coast to Switzerland, had effectively brought war to a grinding halt. Until some way could be found of providing mobile, protected fire support for the attacker, this impasse could not be broken.

Before World War I there had been a number of designs proposed for bizarre-looking mechanical devices in both Britain and France, but all had been summarily discounted or pigeon-holed. These included a tracked armoured vehicle using Diplock caterpillar tracks and another, the "Big Wheel", which was propelled along by three enormous wheels. Ad hoc armoured vehicles were also produced by bolting sheet armour plate on to early motor cars and were used to rescue downed British pilots from behind enemy lines and for light "cavalry" raids by the Belgian Army. Foremost of these

ABOVE: **Wooden model of the "War Machine" as taken from Leonardo da Vinci's notebook. The model was something of a guess as Leonardo never actually built it. Motive power was to be provided by a man inside turning a handle that can be seen connected to the axles, so its engine power was "one manpower"! This model was on show at the Israeli Tank Museum at Latrun, but has now been dismantled.** BELOW: **The "Big Wheel" project must have seemed like something out of H.G. Wells'** *War of the Worlds.* **It was designed to move an armoured vehicle forward on huge 12.2m/40ft diameter wheels, but was never completed. The man in the bowler hat is William Tritton, managing director of William Foster's who would build the first tanks.**

inventors was a British Royal Engineer officer, Ernest Swinton, whose proposal was for an armoured vehicle using American Holt farm-tractor caterpillar tracks for cross-country propulsion. Fortunately Swinton had the backing of Winston Churchill, then First Lord of the Admiralty, otherwise his "landship" might never have seen the light of day. Instead, a Landships

> "And the Lord was with Judah, and he drove out the inhabitants of the mountain, but he could not drive out the inhabitants of the valley, because they had chariots of iron."
> Judges, Chapter 1, Verses 19 and 20

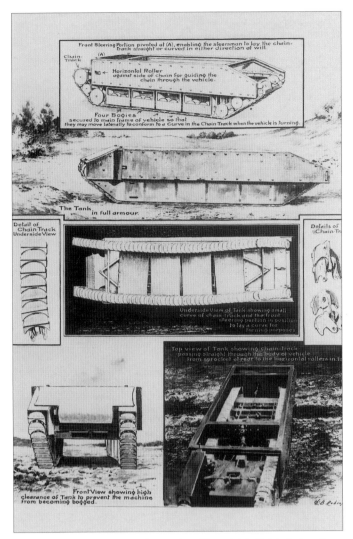

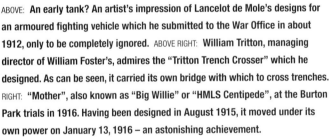

ABOVE: **An early tank? An artist's impression of Lancelot de Mole's designs for an armoured fighting vehicle which he submitted to the War Office in about 1912, only to be completely ignored.** ABOVE RIGHT: **William Tritton, managing director of William Foster's, admires the "Tritton Trench Crosser" which he designed. As can be seen, it carried its own bridge with which to cross trenches.** RIGHT: **"Mother", also known as "Big Willie" or "HMLS Centipede", at the Burton Park trials in 1916. Having been designed in August 1915, it moved under its own power on January 13, 1916 – an astonishing achievement.**

"The structure of the machine in its early stages being boxlike, some term conveying the idea of a box or container seemed appropriate. We rejected in turn – container – reservoir – cistern. The monosyllable TANK appealed to us as being likely to catch on and be remembered."
The Landships Committee

Committee was formed, chaired by Tennyson d'Eyncourt, Director of Naval Construction, and included remarkable men such as William Tritton, managing director of William Foster and Co. Ltd of Lincoln (the firm that would build the first tanks), Royal Naval Lieutenants Walter Gordon Wilson and Albert Stern, and of course Ernest Swinton.

Designed by Tritton and Wilson, the No. 1 Lincoln Machine (also called the "Tritton Machine"), and later, after a complete track redesign, given its more familiar name of "Little Willie", came into existence on September 18, 1915. Weighing 18 tons, it was to have had a centrally mounted turret although this was never fitted. This was almost immediately superseded by "Big Willie" also known as "HMLS Centipede" or more affectionately as "Mother", despite being a "Male" tank armed with two long-barrelled 6pdr guns ("Females" had only machine-guns). She was completed in January 1916, and

secretly moved to a trials area near Hatfield Park. Here, on February 2, 1916, "Mother" performed magnificently before a VIP audience and again six days later to His Majesty The King, who was also most impressed. One hundred Mark Is were ordered and given the nickname "Tank" because this was thought to be most likely to catch on and to be memorable.

Other nations were also coming to terms with the need for such a weapon system – first and foremost the French, once Colonel Estienne put forward plans to develop a land battleship, the *Cuirasse terrestre*, after witnessing British trials of the Holt tractor towing artillery guns. This led not only to the production of both the Schneider and St Chamond heavy tanks, but also the remarkably effective FT-17 light tank series. The Americans, Italians, Russians and surprisingly even the Germans would drag their heels somewhat, but eventually all the major nations would produce their own versions of the tank.

The tank crew

Like every other crew-served weapon system, a tank is only as good as its crew, which is at all times an integral and indispensable component. The first tanks had of necessity either large crews in heavy tanks – the German A7V topped the bill at eighteen, while the British Mark I and the French Saint Chamond had eight and nine respectively – or small crews of only two or three such as those in the tiny French FT-17 and British Whippet. The average-sized tank during World War II and after would have a crew of four men – a driver, a gunner, a loader/radio operator and a commander. They each had their allotted space in the driving or fighting compartment and were allocated personal hearing and vision devices.

The driver was seated at the front surrounded by his controls and instruments. Sometimes he operated a bow machine-gun, or there was a co-driver seated alongside to do so. The other three crewmen were in the turret/fighting compartment, normally with two on one side of the main armament (gunner in front of commander) and one (loader/ operator) on the other. All were located close to their controls and had dedicated seats, vision and intercommunication devices and access/escape hatches.

Today's tank crew live, eat, sleep and fight in their tank throughout the 24-hour battlefield day, but can and do dismount when necessary. Modern tanks are equipped so that the crew

ABOVE: **Members of the crew of a British Mark V Heavy Tank inspect a captured German 13mm/0.512in anti-tank rifle. Up to and including the Mark IV, the crew was eight men, four of whom were the commander and driving team (including two secondary gearsmen); the other four were gunners/loaders.**
BELOW: **The massive Char 2C had an even larger crew of 12 men, the tank commander having an extremely difficult job controlling them all in action. As well as commanding, he also had to serve the 75mm/2.95in main gun.**

can live on board – eating, sleeping and defecating within a filtered atmosphere so that they do not need to wear NBC (nuclear, biological and chemical) clothing or respirators once inside and pressured up. In the early days, British tank crews

wore chain-mail visors to protect against cuts from spawl (flakes of metal chipped off from bullet strikes outside), while heat, fumes and poisonous gas were other hazards they faced. Modern tanks are now designed to be fought closed down, very different to World War II when commanders normally had to have their heads out. The radio system in a tank provides both inter-communications between crewmen as well as long- and short-distance external communications.

Although an individual tank can operate alone, it should never do so, and usually functions as part of a troop or platoon of three or four tanks, or in a larger subunit or unit. Furthermore, tank formations should not operate in isolation, needing infantry, engineer and other all-arms support, especially when holding ground by night, or when operating in urban areas.

Traditionally, tank crews have been all-male, although there were a few cases of women crew members serving in the Red Army during World War II, and there is now an increasing trend towards integration. In some cases, robotic accessories can also take the place of crew members – the most obvious being an automatic loader for the weapon system. While this usually works well, it does inevitably mean that there is one less person to carry out the many and varied other crew tasks such as replenishing ammunition, fuel and rations, gun cleaning, basic maintenance and even the simple yet essential tasks of mounting guard and radio watch, cooking and making the cups of tea or coffee, without which no tank crewman can survive!

"Tank aces" occur in any conflict; however, it is always difficult to single out an individual for special praise because a tank crew lives and fights as a team, and it is this teamwork that wins battles. However, there can be little doubt that the tank commander has the most difficult job, especially if he is commanding other tanks as well as his own, maybe at troop, squadron or regimental level. This requires him to listen constantly on the radio via his headphones (which are now built into his helmet), read a map, guide the driver, locate targets, give fire orders to the gunner, specify what type of ammunition to load, and a hundred and one other things – all at once!

ABOVE LEFT: **The M3 and M3A1 both had a crew of four. In the two-man turret, the commander had to load the main gun and work the turret radio, so he had plenty to do.** ABOVE: **The PzKpfw III was the mainstay of the German panzer divisions and had a crew of five – three in the turret (commander, gunner and loader), plus driver and radio operator.** BELOW: **The Turan I also had a five-man crew – three in the turret, plus driver and co-driver, manning an 8mm/0.315in machine-gun.**

As warfare becomes more sophisticated, so inevitably do modern tanks, and consequently more skills are needed by all members of tank crews to enable them to survive and to fight effectively. The success of the American and British tank crews in the recent war in Iraq is testament to this continuing ability.

World War I

On August 13, 1916, the first detachment of British tanks left for France, the crews departing from Southampton but, because there was no crane there capable of loading them, the tanks left from Avonmouth. They then moved forward by train to the Somme where the great Allied offensive had opened on July 1, with horrendous casualties (British losses were 60,000 on the first day). The Commander-in-Chief of the British Expeditionary Force, General Sir Douglas Haig, was desperate to find a solution to the mounting casualties and seized on the handful of tanks as a panacea, despite the tanks being initially met with amused tolerance or contemptuous scepticism. Haig's plan was to deploy the available tanks (49 in total) over the entire front in twos and threes.

First tank action

On the morning of September 15, 1916, Zero Hour was at 06:20 hours, the tanks being on the move much earlier to reach the start line in time. Some broke down or were ditched moving forward, so where they did get into action, they were available only in ones or twos. Despite this, the effect upon the battle was out of all proportion to their number. Typical were the exploits of D 17 (Dinnaken) of 3 Section, D Company, which was reported in the British Press as "walking up the High Street of Flers with the British Army cheering behind!". German war correspondents were more dramatic: "One stared and stared as if one had lost the power of one's limbs," wrote one, "the monsters approached slowly, hobbling, rolling and rocking, but they approached. Nothing impeded them;

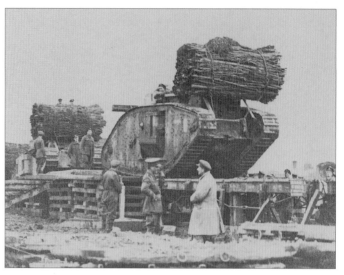

ABOVE: **Moving up for the Battle of Cambrai. British Mark IV heavy tanks, belonging to 4 Battalion, at the Plateau Railhead. Note that they have brushwood fascines (to help in trench crossing) on their fronts and unditching beams on their rears.** BELOW: **Into battle. A British Mark I heavy tank advances, with infantry on foot behind its tail-wheels. This was a device to help with steering but was soon discarded because the wheels fell into shell-holes or trenches, thus proving more a hindrance rather than a help.**

a supernatural force seemed to impel them on. Someone in the trenches said, 'The devil is coming,' and the word passed along the line like wildfire."

Cambrai

Unfortunately their very success worked against them and they continued to be deployed in small numbers for over a year, normally on appalling mud, the thick morass being so bad that tank officers took to carrying long ash sticks to test the depth

in front of their tanks. Eventually Haig allowed Brigadier Hugh Elles, who had taken over command of the Tank Corps from Swinton, to plan a battle on ground of his own choosing. The result was that on November 20, 1917, the entire Tank Corps of 476 tanks took part in the Battle of Cambrai, with Elles in the lead tank, flying the Tank Corps colours from his ash plant.

Zero Hour was 06:00 hours, and after ten hours the battle was won as far as the Tank Corps was concerned; the most rapid advance of the entire war had been achieved at minimal cost – only some 6,000 casualties instead of the anticipated 250,000 or more. Had the British been able to take advantage of this remarkable breakthrough, then a great victory might have been achieved – a remarkable feat by just 690 officers and 3,500 men of the Tank Corps. The Tank Corps had proved itself beyond all expectations, Haig writing in his dispatches that "the great value of the tanks had been conclusively proved".

Five months earlier, however, at Berry au Bac, Estienne's fledgling French tank arm had fought its first battle with 132 Schneiders taking part, but unfortunately involving a long approach march in full view of the enemy. The French tanks quickly encountered heavy artillery fire and many obstacles, 76 tanks being lost without much success. The Germans concluded that tanks were not very effective weapons – a conclusion they would live to regret! One of the main reasons for such heavy losses was the Schneider's vulnerability to the new German "K" anti-tank bullet, but this failure was to make the French concentrate their efforts on the highly successful light FT-17 two-man tanks.

Despite continuing British success, the Germans were slow in appreciating the potential of the new weapon system. However the Americans, who entered the war in April 1917, formed a special board to look into their employment, concluding that the tank was destined to become an important element in the war. They formed a separate tank corps, equipped with a mixture of British heavy and French light tanks. First to make his name in the new corps was a young cavalry captain, George S. Patton, Jnr, destined to become a famous tank commander in World War II.

TOP: **A battlefield scene showing American "doughboys" advancing across enemy trenches, with tank support from the ubiquitous FT-17s.** ABOVE: **A good rear view of a column of Medium Mark A Whippet tanks pausing on its way forward. No doubt the infantry who were passing would have liked a ride!** BELOW: **Two crew members of a British Mark V heavy tank talking to an infantryman. This is of course a modern-day re-enactment at the Tank Museum Bovington, Dorset, England, but the crew members are wearing authentic khaki overalls and the composite/leather crew helmets (affectionately known as "Dead Tortoises"), while their chain-mail face masks (to prevent cuts from spawl) are hanging around their necks.**

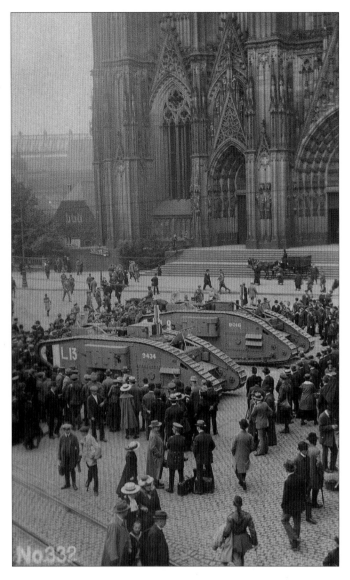

ABOVE: **"Goodbye to boots and saddles!" An M2A4 light tank passes a column of horse-mounted cavalry during exercises in the USA during 1940.** LEFT: **British Army of Occupation in Germany. Taken in 1919, these two Mark V tanks of 12th Battalion Tank Corps are seen outside Cologne Cathedral, on their way to the station to welcome General Petain who was visiting that day.** BELOW: **"Thank God for the French Army!" French AMR 33 light tanks on parade in Paris on Bastille Day, June 14, 1935, when President Lebrun took the salute. France had more tanks than Germany at the start of World War II, but they were still deployed using the old fashioned infantry tactics and spread out in "penny packets", unable to stand up to the new German Blitzkrieg.**

Between the wars

B etween September 1916 and November 1918, British tanks took part in 3,060 separate engagements, French in 4,356 and American in 250, so it is not surprising that one German historian commented that they had been defeated "not by the genius of Marshal Foch, but by 'General Tank'". Despite their successes, the tanks were in for some lean years following World War I, principally due to cost, but also as a result of prejudice against all things mechanical. The British Tank Corps was reduced from 25 battalions when the Armistice was signed to five just a year later. Not until 1922 was a firm decision made to retain a permanent British Tank Corps, while the Americans abolished theirs completely and subjugated their tanks under infantry control. They fared a little better in France, where their tank arm was retained, but seen only as support for the all-powerful infantry, while the cavalry re-emerged, despite their proven battlefield vulnerability.

Apart from the tank element of the British Army of Occupation in Germany, the only exciting episode was the "Russian Stunt", when British tanks were sent to southern

> "The Germans were beaten … not by the genius of Marshal Foch but by 'General Tank'."
> German historian Gen der Infanterie AWH von Zwehl

Russia to help fight against the Bolsheviks, the tank once again showing its prowess – a single tank capturing an entire city. Remarkably the city was Tsaritsin, renamed Stalingrad after the Revolution, which an entire German Army could not capture during World War II.

The 1920s was a great time for armoured theorists, especially in the UK, where Fuller and Liddell Hart produced a stream of books on the theory and practice of armoured warfare. Most remained ignored at home but were avidly read abroad, especially by the Germans. While British, American and French tank soldiers had to fight against the anti-armour prejudice pervading their respective armies, the Germans, despite the crippling restraints of the Versailles Treaty, secretly planned for the future, designing tanks and forming tank units to man them. In Britain prejudice was eventually overcome and mechanization began slowly in 1926, still to be incomplete at

the outbreak of World War II. There was no shortage of able tank designers with men such as Martel in the UK designing cheap, small tanks ideal for training, and J. Walter Christie in the United States creating a revolutionary suspension which allowed high-speed cross-country movement.

The newly emerging Soviet Union did not take an interest in tank development until the start of their first "Five Year Plan" in 1929, thereafter building large numbers of poorly designed tanks. Stalin hindered their armoured development when he carried out his savage purges, removing many of those who had been advocating the theories of Fuller and Liddell Hart. Covertly the Soviets also helped the Germans by allowing them to send prototypes of their new tanks to the secret tank testing ground at Kazan.

When Hitler came to power he quickly realized the potential of the tank and by 1934, having thrown aside all pretence of obeying the Versailles Treaty, began tank-building on a large scale. He created the *Panzerwaffe* (Tank Arm), the first three panzer divisions being formed on October 15, 1935. Their organization bore a close resemblance to the British experimental armoured force of 1927. Officers and men of these divisions would gain useful combat experience as

ABOVE: **Hitler reviews his panzer troops. This scene is in pre-war Berlin, where any excuse for a military parade – such as Hitler's birthday, heroes' memorial days and foreign visitors – was snapped up. Here, Hitler is inspecting his big six-wheeled armoured cars and troop carriers, but on the other side of the Platz are the panzers and crews in their distinctive black uniforms.**

"volunteers" in the German Condor Legion, fighting for General Franco during the Spanish Civil War. It was during this time that the new tactics of *Blitzkrieg* (Lightning War) were perfected, which soon came to revolutionize the battlefield, employing innovative elements such as air–ground support, with dive-bombers and tank formations working closely together. Much of their tactics and training was based on the teachings of General Heinz Guderian, the armoured guru, who had been the first to realize that the panzer division would be the weapon of decision in the new German Army. He visualized armoured forces which did not only contain tanks, but a mix of all fighting arms and services, thus differing from the "all-tank" theories of Fuller and from the policy of tying tanks to infantry as adopted by the French and Americans. His new panzer arm would be the primary striking force in the coming war, and not just a supporting player.

Blitzkrieg!

On September 1, 1939, two German Army Groups swept across the Polish frontier, spearheaded by two Panzer Corps, their aim being to encircle and destroy the Polish Army in a gigantic pincer movement. Germany knew the Poles would fight stubbornly, buoyed up by promises of British and French support. However, unbeknown to Poland and her allies, there was a Nazi–Soviet Pact in which Poland was to be divided in two, the Russians attacking from the rear.

The Germans unleashed a new tactical system on the Poles, perfected by Guderian, which pierced the enemy's front and then encircled and destroyed all or part of their forces. Its key elements were surprise, speed of manoeuvre, shock action from both ground and air, and the retention of battlefield initiative. It required that all commanders used their initiative to the full. Reconnaissance elements led, accompanied by Artillery Forward Observers and Luftwaffe Forward Air Controllers, who could quickly call for fire support. Having located the enemy main positions, the reconnaissance would bypass these strong-points and quickly press on to maintain momentum. They were in constant radio communication with the force commander who controlled the speed of advance, deciding whether the whole force should bypass enemy positions or engage them. The *Schwerpunkt* ("centre of gravity") of the assault was where the commander, being well forward, decided was the best point to attack. Overwhelming force was then concentrated against this point, as Guderian put it, "*Klotzen nicht Kleckern!*" ("Thump them hard, don't pat them!"). The aim of this initial attack was to punch a hole through their lines, to be immediately followed by another element of the force that would pass through and press on,

ABOVE: **At the Channel Coast. The date is May 20, 1940, the place Dunkirk, the tank a PzKpfw 38(t) built by the Czechs and "appropriated" by the Germans.**
BELOW: **Blitzkrieg in action! In the suburbs of Warsaw, a column of German tanks, led by a PzKpfw II Ausf F, passes a 7.5cm/2.95in infantry gun as they batter their way into the city, September 1939.**

avoiding main enemy positions, creating havoc in their rear. Following this up would be motorized infantry, who would "mop up" any remaining resistance, ensuring that the gap was permanent. Such operations demanded teamwork, good communications, command and control, and where possible, surprise. There were no more massive build-ups, long artillery barrages or set-piece attacks which gave the enemy time to prepare. Instead, the overwhelmingly powerful attacking force would hit without warning, smashing through on a narrow front. No wonder Guderian's nickname was *Schnelle Heinz* ("Hurrying Heinz")!

Blitzkrieg was repeated on May 10, 1940, when the Germans invaded the Low Countries and then crossed the Meuse into France. The disorganized and demoralized French

FAR LEFT: **On into Russia! A column of PzKpfw III Ausf Es leaving a ruined Russian village as they head for the steppes.**
LEFT: **The prime architect of the German Blitzkrieg tactics was General Heinz Guderian, seen here during pre-war training.**
BELOW: **The All Arms team was one of the vital components of the German Blitzkrieg. The infantry had to work closely with tanks, as shown here, where they use a tank to get them nearer to the enemy. However, they will have to dismount once the action begins, so that the tank can traverse its turret and engage targets.**

had their armour spread out in "penny packets" and were no match for the German assault, while the British Expeditionary Force (BEF) soon struggled to escape over the Channel. However, a few important challenges to the German offensive occurred, most notably at Arras where a counter-attack by the 4th and 7th Royal Tank Regiments held up the panzers long enough to prevent the BEF from being cut off from their escape ports. By June 18, Paris had capitulated, followed by the complete surrender of France on June 24. The *Panzerwaffe* was in the ascendancy.

Operation "Barbarossa"

Just under a year later, on June 22, 1941, the Germans unleashed three massive army groups against their erstwhile Soviet ally. Similar to the campaigns in Poland and France, panzers spearheaded the German forces, with a front line extending 3,219km/2,000 miles from the Baltic to the Black Sea. The Red Army retreated everywhere, losing more than 3,000 tanks. By autumn the Germans had advanced 885km/

550 miles and occupied 1.3 million sq km/500,000sq miles of Soviet territory, inflicting 2.5 million casualties on the Red Army and capturing over a million prisoners.

On the other side of the world, the USA had begun to awaken, and its massive armaments and tank-building industry swung into action, anticipating its entry into the war. This would change the US Army into the most mechanized force in the world. The British were grateful to receive American tanks to boost their armoured divisions because they were still bedevilled with tank design problems, having too many models that were under-armoured, under-gunned and restricted by turret rings too small to take larger calibre weapons.

Elsewhere, other countries, such as Axis partners Italy and Japan, began increasing their tank-building programmes, but were never very successful. Commonwealth tank development also played its part, although the Allies were to rely on the industrial output of the USA to build the tanks they needed for their armoured forces. On every battlefield, the tank had begun to play a more pivotal role than ever before.

Tanks in other theatres

O f all the unlikely places for tanks to prove their abilities, the barren Western Desert of North Africa was probably the strangest. Yet despite problems caused by the extremes of heat and cold, combined with the effect of sand and grit on their engines and running gear (let alone on their crews), tanks once again proved themselves the dominant arm, this time in desert warfare. Initially it was British tanks against Italian that would capture the headlines, the Matilda II swiftly earning the title "Queen of the Desert". The Italian invasion of Egypt and their subsequent trouncing by a much smaller British and Commonwealth force culminated in the surrender of the entire 10th Italian Army at Beda Fomm, Libya, in February 1941. Here the British 7th Armoured Division (the "Desert Rats") took 20,000 prisoners, together with immense quantities of vehicles, arms and ammunition, for the loss of just nine killed, fifteen wounded and four tanks knocked out.

However, the British would not have it all their own way for long, once General Erwin Rommel and his *Deutsches Afrika Korps* (DAK) arrived. The "Desert Fox", as he was called by both sides, soon proved that he was in his element in the desert, leading from the front and dominating battles by his sheer personality. Hard-fought campaigns then took place

> "We have already reached our first objective which we weren't supposed to get to until the end of May ... You will understand that I can't sleep for happiness."
> Rommel in a letter home to his wife

TOP: **"Queen of the Desert". The British Matilda Mark II was far superior to any of the Italian tanks in the Western Desert because its protection was far better.**

ABOVE: **Across the steppes. Blasting their way through Russian defences, the panzers initially made good progress on the wide open steppes until winter set in.**

from one end of the Western Desert to the other between March 1941 and October 1942. The turning point came with the Battle of El Alamein, Egypt, which gave victory to General Montgomery and his British 8th Army. The DAK then fought a stubborn withdrawal action all the way back to Tunisia, where they were finally forced to surrender on May 12, 1943.

The Japanese bombed Pearl Harbor on December 7, 1941, and in so doing brought the USA into the war, switching their enormous armaments industry to full-scale production. Over 88,400 tanks were built during the war years, nearly four times the production of Germany or Britain. The American armed forces soon numbered over 12 million and a goodly proportion of these fought the Japanese in the Pacific "island-hopping" campaigns that saw tanks being used in a wide variety of new roles. In other parts of the Far East, British and Commonwealth armour fought in unlikely jungle settings, winning victories where tanks were not expected to be able to survive, let alone operate.

From mid-1943, the tide had turned against the Axis powers in nearly every theatre of the war, nowhere more so than on the Russian steppes where the Red Army was able to employ its excellent new tanks – the T-34 and KV-1 – built in ever larger numbers at factories that had been moved safely eastwards. Soon they turned the tables on the overstretched Nazis and were pushing them inexorably back to the Fatherland, in the process winning some enormous tank battles such as the one at Kursk in July–August 1943.

In the Mediterranean theatre, tanks also played a major part in the conquest of Sicily and Italy. In north-west Europe, with the opening of the Second Front on D-Day, June 6, 1944, specialized armour in the form of the Funnies was used to great effect in these landings. Once a breakout from the beaches had been achieved, tanks led the way on all fronts with armoured commanders such as General Patton racing to go further and faster than his fellow generals, giving the Germans no opportunity to regroup.

Nevertheless, the Germans still had a surprise up their sleeve with their heavy armour playing a major role in a totally unexpected counter-attack through the Ardennes region in a conflict which became known as the "Battle of the Bulge".

TOP: "*Panzer Rollen in Afrika Vor!*" A PzKpfw IV belonging to the *Deutsches Afrika Korps* negotiates a sand dune in the North African desert.
ABOVE LEFT: The Red Army resists. Russian medium tanks pressing the Germans back towards Rostov during the autumn of 1942. ABOVE: A US Marine Corps Sherman M4A2 medium tank operating deep in the jungle of Cape Gloucester. Tanks proved their worth in jungles all over the Pacific theatre, being used to great effect by both the US Army and USMC.

This nearly succeeded in breaking through the Allied forces, but proved to be a last gasp, and Allied tanks were soon hammering on the gates of Berlin from all sides. Following Hitler's suicide, Germany sued for peace, surrendering unconditionally on May 7, 1945. Fighting in the Pacific would take a further three months to force Japan into a similar surrender on August 14, bringing World War II to a close.

Would the atom bomb, which had so dramatically heralded in the nuclear age, lead to the demise of the tank?

Wartime development

As World War II progressed, most major tank-building nations produced larger, more powerful, better armed and better armoured tanks. The UK, once the world leader, had been left woefully far behind by the others with tanks that were under-equipped and ill-prepared for the Blitzkrieg tactics of modern war. Their machine-gun armed light tanks were suitable only for peacetime training or possibly reconnaissance tasks, a role soon to be taken over by armoured cars. Likewise, the cruiser and infantry tanks mounted either a tiny 2pdr high velocity anti-tank gun or a 75mm/2.95in close support howitzer. The former was adequate in the anti-armour role but of little use firing High-Explosive (HE) in support of infantry. Unfortunately, the diameter of their turret rings was mainly too small to allow the mounting of larger-calibre weapons. German tanks did not suffer from this design fault. The PzKpfw IIIs and PzKpfw IVs, designed in the early 1930s and forming the backbone of the *Panzerwaffe*, were still in quantity production in the early 1940s, well able to be up-armoured and up-gunned.

The Americans had recognized the need for a dual-purpose main tank armament and the advantages of stabilizing the gun platform so as to hit targets on the move – in most tank versus tank battles the one who hit first usually won. The introduction of American Medium M3 Lee/Grants into British service in the North African desert was the first time they had had a tank gun of this size with dual capability since the naval 6pdr of the Heavy Mark V in World War I. Despite this advantage, the 75mm/2.95in gun remained in service far too long, not being replaced by the much improved 76mm/2.99in gun until later in the war. The British did not produce a real match-winner until the A34 Comet, with its excellent 77mm/3.03in gun, which entered service in March 1945.

ABOVE: **The backbone of the panzer divisions for many years was the PzKpfw IIIs and IVs. This interesting line-up shows (from left to right) Pz IV Ausf F, Pz III Ausf L/M, Pz III Ausf H and Pz IV Ausf F, taken in March 1944.**
BELOW LEFT: **The deeper the Germans penetrated into the Soviet Union, the farther east the Soviets had to move their tank-building factories, like this one that was producing their new heavy tank, the KV-1.**

Although the Germans mostly led the field in tank design – with obvious exceptions such as the Soviet T-34, probably the best all-round tank of the war – they could not match the Americans or the Russians in mass production output. Curiously, they squandered much of their precious production capacity on building ever larger tanks. They created behemoths such as the 68-ton King Tiger, 70-ton Jagdtiger and the last of which was too late to see combat, the 180-ton Maus. These tanks were very difficult to manoeuvre, slow, needed specially reinforced bridging and guzzled fuel, although they could see off every other tank they met with ease. Had they concentrated on producing the PzKpfw V Panther, things might have been different.

Protection became more of a problem as anti-tank weapons improved and the means of penetrating armour became more varied. In addition to conventional Kinetic Energy penetration by solid shot, a new method, High-Explosive Anti-Tank (HEAT) was introduced, which relied on the chemical energy generated

by a high-velocity, high-temperature jet of HE. This was fired at low velocity and was thus most accurate at shorter ranges in hand-held weapons such as the bazooka. This led to the fitting of "stand-off" armour to protect suspensions and turrets, while front glacis and turret frontal arcs became ever thicker. Other methods of protection included painting with anti-magnetic mine paste (*Zimmerit*) and fitting local smoke dischargers, which fired a pattern of local smoke allowing a tank to escape to cover. Internal protection was improved by not storing ammunition above the turret ring (apart from ready rounds) and by fitting ammunition bins with water jackets.

Engine and track performance also improved, but in many cases petrol engines still had to be used instead of the more robust (and less inflammable) diesels because the majority of diesel fuel was needed for the navies. "Duckbills" (track extensions) were fitted in some cases to improve traction in muddy conditions, while the ingenious Culin Hedgerow Cutter, a device that could cut its way through the thick *bocage* hedgerows of Normandy, won a medal for the American NCO who invented it.

Undoubtedly the biggest continual threat to tanks came from the air in the form of specialized "tank busters" or *Jabos* (*Jagdbombers*), constantly searching out and destroying tank columns, a particular problem for the Germans thanks to the Allies' almost complete air superiority.

TOP: **As well as tank crews, technicians had to learn about new tanks as they came into service – like these REME (Royal Electrical and Mechanical Engineers) craftsmen removing the 75mm/2.95in gun and mantlet from this US M24 Chaffee, the last of the American light tank line of World War II.**
ABOVE: **Stand-off armour. As can be seen on this German PzKpfw III, side plates to protect the suspension and turret sides give the tank improved protection against HEAT (High-Explosive Anti-Tank) projectiles.** BELOW: **Light tanks had to be able to be carried in gliders to support airborne operations. Here a 7-ton British Light Tank Mark VII Tetrarch exits from the nose of a glider.**

The Funnies

Crucial to the success of the Allied armies landing on the Normandy beaches was the support they had from all manner of specialized armour. The driving force behind these strange devices – the product of many inventive minds – was one man, arguably the greatest trainer of British armoured soldiers: Major-General Percy Hobart. He had already proved his prowess before World War II on Salisbury Plain and then in Egypt where he turned the Cairo Mobile Division into the world-famous 7th Armoured Division – the original "Desert Rats" – and following this by forming and training the formidable 11th Armoured Division. However, the 79th Armoured Division, "Hobo's Funnies" (although he detested the nickname), was his crowning achievement.

Strange-looking tanks, fitted with deep-water wading screens, mine-clearing flails, portable bridges, flamethrowers or tank-borne searchlights, joined the more conventional armoured bulldozers and armoured engineers assault vehicles to provide the fire support and assist more conventional tanks over and through the natural and man-made beach obstacles. The Division went on playing an important role right up to and over the Rhine Crossing, when it had a strength of 21,000 all ranks and 1,566 tracked vehicles (compared with 14,000 men and 350 AFVs in a normal armoured division), but always operating in "penny packets" spread across the front line. "Hobo's eagle-eye" appeared to be everywhere, and his contribution to the Allied success was enormous.

As the photographs here and in the directory section show, the majority of Funnies were based upon either the highly adaptable American Sherman M4 Medium Tank or the equally versatile British A22 Churchill Infantry Tank Mark IV. Before the

TOP: **The Churchill "Crocodile" Flamethrower was a fearsome weapon that was still in service in the 1950s. In fact, a squadron's worth went to Korea with the Commonwealth Division as part of the United Nations force, but were only ever used as gun tanks.** ABOVE: **A Sherman DD enters the water during training before D-Day. Note the propellers on the rear (run off the engine and yet to be lowered) and the raised canvas screen which gives the tank the necessary buoyancy.**

LEFT: **The 79th Armoured Division, "Hobo's Funnies", took a bull's head as its insignia.**

formation and equipping of 79th Armoured Division, there had been some limited specialized armour, mainly used in the Middle East, such as Matilda and Valentine-based mine-sweeping tanks, the Matilda nightfighting searchlight (known as the Canal Defence Light) and the Valentine amphibious tank (using a collapsible screen and fitted with Duplex Drive propellers to enable it to swim). These clearly led on to the Sherman/Churchill derivatives that were much improved versions of the originals. Here are some of the most widely used Funnies.

Sherman DD (Duplex Drive)

First ashore with the leading troops was a Sherman gun tank fitted, like the Valentine, with DD propellers and a collapsible screen. Unfortunately, those on the American beaches were launched too far out and many sank before they could reach shore. However, on the British and Canadian beaches they landed successfully and proved invaluable.

LEFT: **A Churchill gun tank uses a Churchill Great Eastern Ramp to surmount an extra high wall.**
BELOW LEFT: **One of the very few Sherman DDs left in existence is this one on show at the Tank Museum, Bovington, as part of the D-Day exhibits.**
BELOW: **A Churchill AVRE (Armoured Vehicle Royal Engineers) fitted with a fascine carrier and brushwood fascine ready to be dropped into any ditch or crater that blocked its way.** BOTTOM: **One of the most successful mine-clearing devices was the Sherman Flail (British designation: the Sherman Crab) that used flails attached to a front-mounted spinning drum to literally blast the mines out of the ground or set them off.**

Sherman Crab

This was again a Sherman gun tank fitted with a flail mine-sweeping device which could sweep a safe lane through a minefield, wide enough to allow tanks and other vehicles to negotiate it in safety.

Churchill AVRE (Armoured Vehicle Royal Engineers)

These were Churchill Mark III or IV tanks, modified to mount a 290mm/11.42in spigot mortar, together with other devices such as various bridges, Bobbin "carpet-layers", fascines and mine exploders. The spigot mortar was used to destroy pill-boxes and was known as a "Flying Dustbin".

Churchill ARKs

A turret-less Churchill tank, modified to carry ramps for use in obstacle crossing. The Germans were completely surprised by these strange-looking vehicles which had no counterpart in the German Army. The Funnies accomplished many tasks on D-Day, including crossing sea walls and anti-tank ditches; breaching sea walls and other obstacles; knocking out gun

emplacements and defended buildings; filling ditches and craters with fascines or crossing them with tank bridges.

After D-Day other Funnies were brought into action, such as Churchill "Crocodile" Flamethrowers, "Kangaroo" armoured personnel carriers (based on Ram tanks) and other types of bridges, bulldozers, etc. No wonder they were called the "tactical key to victory".

On to victory!

Once the Rhine was crossed, with armour leading on all fronts, the Allied armies moved deeper and deeper into Germany. Now the lighter, faster American mediums and British cruisers really came into their own, their speed, reliability and overwhelming numbers counting for more in the end than the superior enemy firepower and protection. I remember being told of one German tank commander who, having boasted that one Tiger was better than ten Shermans, then smiled ruefully and said, "but you alvays haff eleven!" Nevertheless it was no easy ride, especially with the added danger from a proliferation of hand-held anti-tank weapons, such as the *Panzerfaust* and *Panzerschreck*. The once proud panzer divisions were by now a shadow of their former selves, yet single Tigers and Panthers still performed miracles until they were taken out by superior numbers or by the dreaded *Jabos*.

The Allies were also fielding better tanks, the American M26 General Pershing heavy tank, with its highly effective 90mm/3.54in M3 gun, had reached Europe in January 1945 and even saw action in the Pacific theatre before the war ended. The highly effective British Comet entered service at about the same time as the Pershing, but unfortunately its successor, the world-beating A41 Centurion, was not in prototype stage until January 1945 with the first six vehicles

ABOVE: **Brilliant British commander Field Marshal Bernard Montgomery always wore a Royal Tank Regiment black beret and badge on to which was sewn his General's badge. "Monty" had his own M3 Grant medium tank in the Western Desert, now in the Imperial War Museum, London.**

ABOVE: **One of the greatest German armoured commanders was Field Marshal Erwin Rommel, who commanded the *Deutsches Afrika Korps* in North Africa, then Army Group B on the Atlantic Wall and Channel Coast. Implicated in the bomb plot against Hitler, he was forced to commit suicide.**

being rushed to Germany for testing in combat conditions in May 1945. This gives a measure of how far behind the British were in the tank development race.

On the Eastern Front the Red Army "Steamroller" moved closer to Berlin, headed by the ubiquitous T-34 and the new JS-1, JS-2 and JS-3, with their 122mm/4.8in gun and thick armour. Particularly deadly was the JS-3 with its new ballistically shaped cast hull and smoothly curved turret, but all were more than a match for their aging opponents.

Tank destroyers

Before closing on World War II it is perhaps relevant to deal here with tank destroyers. All the major tank-building nations employed them because they were an ideal way of getting a

> "Armor, as the ground arm of mobility, emerged from World War II with a lion's share of the credit for the Allied victory. Indeed armor enthusiasts at that time regarded the tank as being the main weapon of the land army."
> US Army Lineage series *Armor-Cavalry*

more powerful anti-armour weapon into battle on a smaller, lighter or almost obsolescent tank chassis, thus prolonging its effective battlefield life. The Americans, however, viewed things slightly differently. Early in the war they had been heavily influenced by the way German tanks had sliced through the opposition in Poland, France and Russia, and this had a bad effect on American morale. They came to the conclusion that the answer was to have masses of fast-moving, high-velocity anti-tank guns whose primary task was to knock out enemy tanks. This led to the creation of Tank Destroyer Command (with their motto "Seek, Strike and Destroy!"), which at its peak in early 1943 contained 106 active tank destroyer battalions – only 13 less than the total number of US tank battalions. From then on, numbers started to decline, principally because the expected massed German tank formations were not used against the Americans, being needed more on the Eastern Front. Nevertheless, the M10 Wolverine, the M18 Hellcat and the M36 tank destroyers all gave useful service in the US Army, while both the British and the Germans made full use of their tank destroyers for many tasks, often in lieu of normal gun tanks. The British up-gunned some of their M10s by installing their 17pdr Mk V gun, the resulting highly effective tank destroyer being known as the "Achilles". Undoubtedly the German *Jagdpanther* was one of the best tank destroyers ever built, while *Jagdtiger* was the heaviest German AFV to go into active service. Smaller tank destroyers, like the Hetzer, which utilized well-proven

TOP LEFT: **One of the smallest number of tanks in any theatre were those of the composite squadron of Light Mark VI and Matilda Mark II on Malta. Note the strange camouflage to blend in with the hundreds of dry stone walls on the island.** TOP RIGHT: **America's most famous armoured general was General George S. Patton, Jr, whose flamboyant style made him instantly recognizable everywhere. This evocative statue of Patton stands at Ettelbruck, Luxembourg.** ABOVE: **Berlin at last! A column of Red Army JS-2 heavy tanks drives through the Brandenburg Gate, sealing the fate of the Third Reich.**

components of the Czech-built PzKpfw 38(t), continued to be used by the Swiss Army long after the end of the war.

"Armor, as the ground arm of mobility, emerged from World War II with a lion's share of the credit for the Allied victory. Indeed armor enthusiasts at that time regarded the tank as being the main weapon of the land army." That is how the US Army Lineage series *Armor-Cavalry* put it, and it would be hard to disagree. "General Tank" had done it again!

A–Z of World War Tanks

1916–45

The size and shape of the first tanks of 1916 depended more upon the need to cross trenches and deal with machine-gun nests than any other factor. Improvements were then rapidly made, the "International" Mark VIII of 1918 being way ahead of the original Mark I, while the tiny French FT-17, which was the first tank with a fully traversing turret, was sought worldwide. From 1918 onwards, financial restrictions put paid to progress among the victors, leaving it to Germany to develop armoured warfare. Tanks like the Panzer III and IV stayed in production for most of World War II, while the Allies floundered, building a plethora of generally inferior models. In the end it was the remarkable transformation of American industry that saved the day, producing vast numbers of reliable, adaptable tanks like the Sherman. Towards the end of World War II, the Soviets also produced some excellent medium and heavy tanks, including perhaps the best Allied tank of all, the T-34. Nevertheless, ask anyone to name the outstanding tank of the war and they will invariably say the German Tiger I, whose dreaded 8.8cm/3.46in gun and thick armour made it feared everywhere.

LEFT: **This British Heavy Mark V of 1918 is still in full running order at the Tank Museum, Bovington, Dorset, despite having seen action on the battlefields of France during World War I.**

A7V Sturmpanzerwagen

At the start of World War I the Germans lacked anyone at ministerial level prepared to put their weight behind any tank projects; consequently no attempt was made to build one until after British tanks had already appeared. Ultimately only one German tank type took part in the war, the A7V, with 100 being ordered but less than a quarter of that number being built.

Weighing 30,480kg/30 tons, this leviathan consisted of a basic massive steel box superstructure built over a tractor chassis. It had a suitably enormous crew of 18, 12 of whom were machine-gunners, divided into pairs, with one team stationed at the rear and the rest along the sides. The main armament was a 5.7cm/2.24in gun mounted in the nose. The A7V's cross-country performance was poor, although it had a top road speed of 14kph/9mph. Despite this and its frightening appearance, it was remarkably ineffective, being both cumbersome and mechanically unreliable.

The first tank versus tank battle took place at Villers Bretonneux, France, on April 24, 1918, when three British tanks (two Female and one Male) met three A7Vs. Two of the enemy were too far away to be engaged, but the British Male, a Mark IV, opened up on the leading A7V. The British tank crews had been badly gassed the previous day, two of the Mark IV Male's crew being evacuated and the remainder still suffering from the effects of the mustard gas. This made it very difficult for the British tank gunners to see properly to engage their enemy.

TOP: **The only surviving A7V is in the Australian War Museum. However, the German Panzer Museum at Munster now has a full-scale replica which is seen here in a panorama setting in their museum.** LEFT: **A captured A7V arriving at Erin near Bermicourt, France, the location of the Tank Corps Central Workshops.**

ABOVE: **Two A7Vs in a village near Villers Bretonneux, France. The vehicles were "Hagen" and "Wotan".** RIGHT: **According to the chalk marking, this A7V was captured by the New Zealanders.** BELOW: **Thirteen of the eighteen-man crew are seen here riding on the outside of the tank – probably to escape from the heat, fumes and noise inside.**

Their first rounds missed, and the A7V quickly replied with armour-piercing machine-gun fire, causing "splash" and sparks inside the British tanks. The German tank engaged the two Female tanks, damaging both and forcing them to withdraw. The British commander of the Male, Second Lieutenant Frank Mitchell then halted his tank to give the gunner a steady shot. They were both delighted to see the A7V keel over, but it had simply run down a steep bank and overturned. This was nevertheless counted as the first tank kill.

A7V Sturmpanzerwagen

Entered service: 1917
Crew: 18
Weight: 30,480kg/30 tons
Dimensions: Length – 8m/26ft 3in
  Height (over turret hatch) – 3.4m/11ft 2in
  Width – 3.2m/10ft 6in
Armament: Main – 5.7cm/2.24in gun
  Secondary – 6 x 7.92mm/0.31in Maxim-Spandau 08/15 machine-guns
Armour: Maximum – 30mm/1.18in
Powerplant: 2 x Daimler-Benz 4-cylinder petrol, 74.5kW/100hp
Performance: Speed – 15kph/9mph
  Range – 60–70km/37–44 miles

A1E1 Independent

In December 1922, the War Office asked Vickers to design a new heavy tank to replace the World War I Mark V. The chosen design was for a tank with a main gun in an all-round traversing turret and machine-guns in four small separate turrets with limited traverse only. The "land warship" idea, pioneered by the British with this tank, would enjoy a brief European-wide popularity before its shortcomings became apparent and the practical problems of command, crew control, weight and size made it redundant.

However, as an experimental model it anticipated and influenced future tank design with various new developments, including: a self-cleaning drive sprocket; an aero-marine inertia starter; a

prototype intercom system using the laryngaphone and mechanical indicators; as well as better battle stations for increased crew comfort and safety.

The controls of the A1E1 were hydraulically operated by the driver at the front, with the engine at the rear and the tracks slung low with the hull between them. Main armament was a 3pdr in the main turret, with four Vickers machine-guns in the subsidiary turrets. Its 296.7kW/398bhp Armstrong-Siddeley V12 engine theoretically gave the A1E1 a road speed of 40kph/25mph, but in practice it was lower (32kph/20mph) because it consumed oil heavily. The engine was also notoriously difficult to start – hence the fitting of the aero-marine inertia starter.

With the weight at 32,514kg/32 tons, the engine, final drive, suspension, rubber tyres of the road wheels and the brakes all gave constant trouble because the tank was too heavy, out of proportion and too long for its width. This in turn made it difficult to steer, and caused serious problems at the rear where the track frames started to peel away from the hull. Eventually after an expensive but useful seven-year development cycle, the project was shelved after costing over £150,000 – a high price at that time.

A1E1 Independent

Entered service: This tank never entered service
Crew: 8
Weight: 32,514kg/32 tons
Dimensions: Length – 7.6m/24ft 11in
  Height (over turret hatch) – 2.72m/8ft 11 in
  Width – 2.67m/8ft 9in
Armament: Main – 3pdr QF (quick-firing) gun
  Secondary – 4 x Vickers machine-guns in subsidiary turrets
Armour: Maximum – 30mm/1.18in
Powerplant: Armstrong-Siddeley air-cooled V12, 296.7kW/398bhp
Performance: Speed – 32kph/20mph
  Range – 150km/93 miles

TOP: **Built in 1926, this multi-turreted, heavily armed British tank was designed, as the name implies, for independent action. Its design was very advanced for the time, and it set a trend for similar tanks in France, Germany and Russia. The only A1E1 built still survives at the Tank Museum, in Dorset. During World War II it was taken out of the Museum and used to guard the approaches to Bovington.**
LEFT: **Internal photograph of the main armament of the Independent.**

A9 Cruiser Tank Mark I

A9 Cruiser Tank Mk I
Entered service: 1938
Crew: 6
Weight: 12,190 kg/12 tons
Dimensions: Length – 5.79m/19ft
Height (over turret hatch) – 2.54m/8ft 4in
Width – 2.54m/8ft 4in
Armament: Main – 2pdr gun
Secondary – 3 x Vickers 7.7mm/0.303in machine-guns (one coaxial, two in separate turrets)
Armour: Maximum – 10–14mm/0.39–0.55in
Powerplant: AEC Type A179 6-cylinder petrol, 111.9kW/150bhp
Performance: Speed – 40kph/25mph
Range – 241km/150 miles

Medium tanks lacked speed, while light tanks lacked both firepower and protection. This led to the design of a series of "Cruiser" tanks, the A9 being the first. Sir John Carden completed the design in 1934, trials started in 1936, and production in 1937. One hundred and twenty-five tanks were built in total, and saw service from 1938–41.

The weight of the A9 being relatively low allowed it to be powered by a commercially available 9.64 litre AEC bus engine, which gave it a top speed of 40kph/25mph. It also had a distinctive "slow-motion" suspension system with the triple-wheel bogies on springs mounted with Newton hydraulic shock absorbers.

It was armed with a 2pdr main gun and three machine-guns, one coaxial in the main turret and the other two in separate auxiliary turrets, and it was the first British tank with an hydraulic-powered turret traverse.

Combat experience in France in 1940 proved that the design had two critical drawbacks: the armour was too thin and the speed too slow for the cruiser role. It also fought in the Western Desert in North Africa, where, although adequate against the Italian armour, it was just too slow and thinly armoured when confronted by contemporary German tanks.

A10 Cruiser Tank Mark IIA

The A10 shared various features with the A9, including the same designer, Sir John Carden. It had the same basic turret and hull shape but with the two secondary turrets removed and additional armour installed by simply bolting extra plates on to the outside of the hull and turret, making it the first British tank built in this composite fashion. One hundred and seventy-five vehicles were ordered and completed by September 1940. A10s were issued to units of the 1st Armoured Division, and were used in France in 1940 and in the Western Desert until late 1941. However, like its predecessor, it was too slow and lightly armoured when confronted by contemporary German tanks.

A10 Cruiser Tank Mk IIA
Entered service: 1940
Crew: 5
Weight: 13,970kg/13.75 tons
Dimensions: Length – 5.51m/18ft 1in
Height (over turret hatch) – 2.59m/8ft 6in
Width – 2.54m/8ft 4in
Armament: Main – 2pdr QFSA (quick-firing semi-automatic) L/52 gun
Secondary – 2 x 7.92mm/0.31in Besa (one coaxial and one hull)
Armour: Maximum – 22–30mm/0.87–1.18in
Powerplant: AEC Type A179 6-cylinder petrol, 111.9kW/150bhp
Performance: Speed – 26kph/16.16mph
Range – 161km/100 miles

LEFT: **Sir John Carden designed the A10 Cruiser Tank Mark II. It was more heavily armoured than its A9 predecessor, and replaced the two separate machine-gun turrets with a single Besa machine-gun. This model has been painted in the original British wartime desert camouflage pattern rather than that used in temperate climates.**

A11 Infantry Tank Mark I Matilda I

The first pilot model of the A11 was designed by Sir John Carden and produced by Vickers in 1936. It had a maximum speed of only 13kph/8mph because at the time it was considered that Infantry tanks were only required to keep up with the infantry as they advanced at a walking pace. It was armed with either a 7.7mm/0.303in or 12.7mm/0.5in machine-gun.

To keep costs to a minimum, the construction was kept very simple. A commercial Ford V8 engine and transmission were installed with the steering, brakes, clutches and suspension adapted from those used in the Vickers Light Tanks and Dragon gun tractors. The body was of an all-riveted construction, with the exception of the turret which was cast.

The first production order for 60 vehicles was placed in April 1937, and later increased to 140, all of which were completed by August 1940. Although they were cheap and reliable, they were soon obsolete – being outgunned from the start. Nevertheless, they did see action in the early days of World War II and thereafter were used for training purposes only.

There are a number of stories as to how the tank got its nickname Matilda, one being that when General Sir Hugh Elles saw the tank's comic, duck-like appearance and gait, he named it after a cartoon series of the day. In fact, the codeword "Matilda" appears on the original proposal for the A11 in John Carden's handwriting.

A11 Infantry Tank Mk I Matilda I	
Entered service: 1938	
Crew: 2	
Weight: 11,160kg/11 tons	
Dimensions: Length – 4.85m/15ft 11in	
Height (over turret hatch) –1.85m/6ft 1in	
Width – 2.29m/7ft 6in	
Armament: 1 x 12.7mm/0.5in or 7.7mm/0.303in	
Vickers machine-gun	
Armour: Maximum – 60mm/2.36in	
Powerplant: Ford V8 petrol, 52.22kW/70bhp	
Performance: Speed – 13kph/8mph	
Range – 129km/80 miles	

TOP: **The small but heavily armoured A11 Infantry Tank Mark I Matilda I. It was invulnerable to anything but the largest enemy anti-tank guns because of its thick armour. However, it was only armed with a single machine-gun, and was very slow.**

LEFT: **A somewhat battle-scarred Matilda I – this model is the A11E1 prototype.**

A12 Infantry Tank Mark II Matilda II

In 1936, design began on the successor to the Matilda I, which was to mount a 2pdr main gun and have an increased road speed of around 16–24kph/10–15mph. It was hoped to modify the A11, but it soon became apparent that this would not be practical. Instead, the new design, designated the A12 Infantry Tank Mark II, would be based on the A7 Medium Tank, and built by the Vulcan Foundry of Warrington. Twin ganged AEC diesel engines and a Wilson epicyclic gear box were installed, and the tank was armed with a coaxially mounted 2pdr and 7.92mm/0.312in Besa machine-gun.

The powered turret could be traversed in 14 seconds using a system adapted from that fitted to the Vickers A9. The hull armour was cast and the tracks were protected by one-piece armour side skirts with five mud chutes.

The Matilda played its most important role in the early Western Desert campaigns. In Libya in 1940, its heavy armour was soon found to be almost immune to Italian anti-tank and tank fire. Until the appearance of the German 8.8cm/3.46in Flak gun in 1941, used in an anti-tank role, it was the most effective of the British tanks.

ABOVE: **The Bovington Tank Museum's A12 Infantry Tank Mark II Matilda. It is painted in the original Western Desert camouflage and named "Golden Miller" in honour of Major General Bob Foote's tank which he commanded when, as Commanding Officer of 7 RTR, he was awarded the Victoria Cross for outstanding courage and leadership over the period from May 27 to June 15, 1942.**

Unfortunately, as the Matilda turret could not fit the 6pdr due to the small size of its turret ring, its importance began to diminish. There were, however, many special purpose variants produced, including:
• Matilda CDL (Canal Defence Light): a powerful searchlight used to illuminate battlefields at night.
• Baron I, II, III and IIIA: flail mine-clearers.
• Matilda Scorpion: flail mine-clearer.
• Matilda with AMRA (Anti-Mine Roller Attachment): mine-clearer using rollers.
• Matilda with Carrot (Carrot demolition charge): 272kg/600lb HE (High-Explosive).
• Matilda Frog: flamethrower developed in Australia.
• Matilda Murray: flamethrower also developed in Australia.

ABOVE RIGHT: **Sandstorm approaching! A Matilda Mark II – the Commanding Officers's tank of 4 RTR – in the desert, alongside his heavy-utility staff car, as a *Khamseen* (dust storm) blows up behind them.**
LEFT: **A Matilda II in the shadow of St Paul's Cathedral, London.**

A12 Infantry Tank Mk II Matilda II

Entered service: 1939
Crew: 4
Weight: 26,924kg /26.5 tons
Dimensions: Length – 5.61m/18ft 5in
  Height (over turret hatch) – 2.52m/8ft 3in
  Width – 2.59m/8ft 6in
Armament: Main – 2pdr OQF (ordnance quick-firing) gun
  Secondary – 1 x coaxial 7.92mm/0.312in Besa machine-gun
Armour: Maximum – 78mm/3.07in
Powerplant: 2 x AEC 6-cylinder diesels, 64.8kW/87bhp
Performance: Speed – 13kph/8mph
  Range – 258km/160 miles

LEFT: **Developed from the high-speed Christie-type BT tanks then in service with the Red Army, the A13 was based on a Christie model imported from the USA. It saw operational service both in France and the Western Desert.**

A13 Cruiser Tank Mark III

The A13 originated in late 1936 after British War Office observers had witnessed the high speed of the Russian Christie-type BT tanks in service with the Red Army. The Nuffield Company was asked to design a similar tank based on the Christie design as a high-speed replacement for the A9 and A10. The A13 was based on an actual Christie vehicle imported from the USA, developed in under two years and in service by 1938. It had the Christie suspension system, a high power-to-weight ratio, and a very high top speed of over 48kph/30mph. The engine could be started electrically or by using compressed air. The simple flat-sided turret gave the tank a distinctive appearance. It was used by the 1st Armoured Division in France 1940 and in small numbers with the 7th Armoured Division in the Western Desert in 1940–41, but was too lightly armoured and under-gunned when compared to its German contemporaries.

A13 Cruiser Tank Mk III

Entered service: 1938
Crew: 4
Weight: 14,225kg/14 tons
Dimensions: Length – 6.02m/19ft 9in
　Height (over turret hatch) – 2.59m/8ft 6in
　Width – 2.54m/8ft 4in
Armament: Main – 2pdr QFSA (quick-firing semi-automatic) gun
　Secondary – 1 x coaxial Vickers 7.7mm/0.303in machine-gun
Armour: Maximum – 14mm/0.55in
Powerplant: Nuffield Liberty V12 petrol, 253.64kW/340bhp
Performance: Speed – 48kph/30mph
　Range – 145km/90 miles

A13 Mark II Cruiser Tank Mark IV

The A13 Mark II was the up-armoured version of the A13 with extra armoured steel plates giving added protection and eliminating shot traps. Hollow "V"-sided plates were added to the original A13 type turret – some A13s were also upgraded to similar standards – and this gave the turret a very distinctive appearance with its faceted sides. Due to the high power-to-weight ratio of the Nuffield Liberty V12 petrol engine, the extra armour did not adversely affect the vehicle's performance. The A13 Mark II was in production in 1938, and used in France in 1940 and in the Western Desert in 1940–41. Features included Christie suspension and varied patterns of mantlet. Some 655 were built in total. Once more it was under-gunned, its 2pdr being a satisfactory anti-tank weapon but far too small when used with HE (High-Explosive) munitions.

LEFT: **The A13 Mark II Cruiser Tank Mark IV was essentially an up-armoured version of the Cruiser Tank Mark III. The excellent power-to-weight ratio meant that the increase in armour had little effect upon its top speed.**

A13 Mk II Cruiser Tank Mk IV

Entered service: 1940
Crew: 4
Weight: 15,040kg/14.8 tons
Dimensions: Length – 6m/19ft 9in
　Height (over turret hatch) – 2.59m/8ft 6in
　Width – 2.59m/8ft 6in
Armament: Main – 2pdr OQF (ordnance quick-firing) L/52 gun
　Mk IVCS (close-support) 94mm/3.7in howitzer
　Secondary – 1 x coaxial 7.7mm/0.303in or 7.92mm/0.312in Besa or 7.7mm/0.303in Vickers machine-gun
Armour: Maximum – 30mm/1.18in
Powerplant: Nuffield Liberty V12 petrol, 253.64kW/340bhp
Performance: Speed – 48kph/30mph
　Range – 145km/90 miles

A13 Mark III Cruiser Tank Mark V Covenanter

Built by the London, Midland and Scottish Railway Company, the Covenanter was based on the A13 Mark II and used many of its parts in order to keep costs down. It had a powerful purpose-built Meadows Flat-12 engine and a low-set Christie suspension. However, a design flaw of this vehicle was the positioning of the engine at the rear while the cooling radiator was placed at the front alongside the driver. As a result, the vehicle was plagued by overheating, causing continual mechanical problems.

It saw service from 1940–43, later versions having a better engine-cooling system, a different mantlet, and a number of other improvements.

However, the Covenanter's problems were never satisfactorily solved. As a result, the vehicle never saw action, but was used in a training role and in the development of variants, including:
• Covenanter CS: close-support version, armed with a 76.2mm/3in howitzer in place of the normal 2pdr.
• Covenanter with AMRA (Anti-Mine Roller Attachment): mine-clearing device pushed in front of the tank in order to set off mines by pressure.

TOP: **An excellent view of an A13 Mark III Cruiser Tank Mark V Covenanter taken during "Battle Day" at Bovington, Dorset. The ill-fated Covenanter was a failure due to engine overheating problems, and it never saw action.** ABOVE: **Despite its stylish appearance, the unhappy Covenanter was never a success and was plagued with mechanical problems. (The Tank Museum's model was dug up some years ago and restored to cosmetic order before going on show.)**

• Covenanter OP (Observation Post), Command: with extra radio equipment and a dummy gun.
• Covenanter Bridgelayer: bridgelayer with 10.36m/34ft bridge.

A13 Mk III Cruiser Tank Mk V Covenanter

Entered service: 1940
Crew: 4
Weight: 18,289kg/18 tons
Dimensions: Length – 5.8m/19ft
　Height (over turret hatch) – 2.24m/7ft 4in
　Width – 2.62m/8ft 7in
Armament: Main – 2pdr OQF (ordnance quick-firing) gun
　Secondary – 1 x coaxial 7.92mm/0.312in Besa machine-gun
Armour: Maximum – 40mm/1.57in
Powerplant: Meadows DAV1 12-cylinder petrol, 223.8kW/300bhp
Performance: Speed – 50kph/31mph
　Range – 161km/100 miles

A15 Cruiser Tank Mark VI Crusader

The Crusader was built by Nuffields utilizing a large number of components from the A13 series, including both the Christie suspension and Liberty engine of the original design, as always to keep down costs, production time and vehicle weight. It too had a riveted hull, welded turret and an extra outer layer of armour bolted on.

Ready by March 1940, production was then increased and a consortium produced 5,300 Crusaders by 1943 as it became the principal British tank from spring 1941 until the arrival of the American Sherman.

However, the Crusader always suffered from poor reliability, which reflected the urgency with which it had been rushed into production. It first saw action near Fort Capuzzo, Libya, in June 1941 and did well against Italian armour, but although the Germans respected its speed, it was no match for the PzKpfw III

or indeed the 5.5cm/2.17in, 7.5cm/2.95in and 8.8cm/3.46in anti-tank guns.

After withdrawal from front-line use in May 1943, it was mainly used for training, but also converted for special purposes, including:

• Crusader OP (Observation Post) and Crusader Command: vehicles modified with dummy gun and extra radio and communications equipment.
• Crusader III, AA (Anti-Aircraft) Marks I/II/III: Mark I – the turret was removed and replaced by single Bofors 40mm/1.57in Anti-Aircraft mount; Mark II – a new enclosed turret with twin 20mm/0.79in Oerlikon AA cannon; Mark III – similar to the AA Mark II but with radio equipment removed from turret and installed in hull.
• Crusader II, Gun Tractor Mk 1: open-topped box superstructure converted as a fast tractor for 17pdr anti-tank gun and its crew.

ABOVE LEFT: **This is the Tank Museum's Crusader III, the final production model, armed with a 6pdr instead of the original 2pdr gun.** ABOVE: **Tank crewmen hard at work. The crew of a Crusader III, belonging to the 16th/5th Royal Lancers cleaning their 6pdr gun in Tunisia, April 1943.**

• Crusader ARV (Armoured Recovery Vehicle): removal of turret and addition of recovery equipment.
• Crusader Dozer: turret removed, winch and jib fitted for working dozer blade.
• Crusader with AMRA (Anti-Mine Roller Attachment): mine-clearer.

LEFT: **Tanks in line! This mixed 8th Army tank column, photographed in the Western Desert, is being led by two Crusaders, the front one being a Crusader IICS (mounting the close-support 76.2mm/3in howitzer instead of a 2pdr). The Crusader was the best of the early cruisers.**

A15 Cruiser Tank Mk VI Crusader

Entered service: 1940
Crew: Mk VI – 5; Mk III – 3
Weight: Mk I/II – 19,255kg/18.95 tons
Mk III – 20, 067kg/19.75 tons
Dimensions: Length – Mk I/II – 5.99m/19ft 8in
Mk III – 6.3m/20ft 8in
Height (over turret hatch) – 2.24m/7ft 4in
Width – 2.64m/8ft 8in
Mk III – 2.79m/9ft 2in
Armament: Main – Mk I/II – 2pdr OQF (ordnance quick-firing) L/52 gun
Mk III – 6pdr OQF gun
Secondary – 1 or 2 x 7.92mm/0.312in Besa machine-guns
Armour: Maximum – 51mm/2.01in
Powerplant: Nuffield Liberty Mk III/IV V12 petrol, 253.64kW/340bhp
Performance: Speed – 44kph/27mph
Range – 161km/100 miles

A17 Light Tank Mark VII Tetrarch

Following on from the light Mark VI family, Vickers built the Tetrarch (originally called Purdah) in 1937. It was accepted by the British Army in 1938, but production was delayed until 1940, by which time it was obsolescent, light tanks having been almost entirely replaced by armoured cars in the reconnaissance role. Eventually, however, about 180 were built, some being sent to the USSR (Lend-Lease),

while a squadron's worth saw action in Madagascar in May 1942. They proved unsuitable for the desert (due to inadequate cooling), but were given a new lease of life in 1943 when adopted for use as an air-portable tank to support airborne forces (the Hamilcar glider being specially designed to carry it). Some saw action on D-Day and others at the Rhine Crossing. A few were converted to perform a close-support role mounting

a 76.3mm/3in howitzer instead of the usual 2pdr. The Tetrarch's unique feature was its new suspension with large road wheels which could be partially skid-steered to improve turning.

LEFT: **Designed in 1937 as a private venture, the A17 Light Tank Mark VII Tetrarch came into its own with the development of airborne forces. An airborne reconnaissance regiment was specially formed as a part of 6th Airborne Division for the Normandy invasion. Tetrarchs remained in service until 1949 when the Hamilar glider, which had been designed to carry them, was withdrawn from service.**

A17 Light Tank Mk VII Tetrarch

Entered service: 1942
Crew: 3
Weight: 7,620kg/7.5 tons
Dimensions: Length – 4.11m/13ft 6in
 Height (over turret hatch) – 2.12m/6ft 11.5in
 Width – 2.31m/7ft 7in
Armament: Main – 2pdr QFSA (quick-firing semi-automatic) gun
 Secondary – 1 x coaxial 7.92mm/0.312in Besa machine-gun
Armour: Maximum – 14mm/0.55in
Powerplant: Meadows MAT 12-cylinder petrol, 123kW/165bhp
Performance: Speed – 64kph/40mph
 Range – 225km/140 miles

A25 Light Tank Mark VIII Harry Hopkins

Last of the Vickers Light series and originally known as Tank, Light Mark VII, revised, this model underwent two more changes in name – officially being called the Mark VIII but more colloquially Harry Hopkins after the American President Roosevelt's confidential advisor. Although there were improvements, including a revised faceted hull and

turret, thicker armour and hydraulically assisted steering, the Harry Hopkins was still small, unreliable and vulnerable when compared to the opposition. It was perhaps just as well that it was destined never to see action.

Instead, some were used as the basis for the Alecto dozer and other self-propelled gun projects mounting:

a 95mm/3.74in howitzer (Alecto I); a 6pdr (Alecto II); a 25pdr howitzer (Alecto III); and a 32pdr (Alecto IV) – although only the first two were actually built, and none entered service.

LEFT: **The A25 Light Tank Mark VIII Harry Hopkins was designed as a successor to the Tetrarch. Although some 100 were built in 1944, they were never used in action. The Alecto Dozer had a hydraulically operated dozer blade in place of the gun mount, so it was turretless.**

A25 Light Tank Mk VIII Harry Hopkins

Entered service: 1944
Crew: 3
Weight: 8,636kg/8.5 tons
Dimensions: Length – 4.27m/14ft
 Height (over turret hatch) – 2.11m/6ft 11in
 Width – 2.71m/8ft 10.5in
Armament: Main – 2pdr OQF (ordnance quick-firing) gun
 Secondary – 1 x 7.92mm/0.312in Besa machine-gun
Armour: Maximum – 38mm/1.5in
Powerplant: Meadows 12-cylinder petrol, 110.3kW/148bhp
Performance: Speed – 48kph/30mph
 Range – 201km/125 miles

A22 Infantry Tank Mark IV Churchill

The Churchill was the first British tank to be completely designed during World War II, and was in production throughout the conflict. The earliest model was built in 1941, armed with a 2pdr gun in the turret and a 76.2mm/3in close-support howitzer in its nose. With thick armour and a good cross-country performance (albeit slow), it was undoubtedly one of the best and most well-liked British tanks of the war. It was also the first British tank to mount the US 75mm/2.95in gun – the guns and mantlets being salvaged from knocked-out Shermans in Tunisia.

With less than 100 tanks in the UK after Dunkirk, the A22 was built hurriedly by a consortium of companies, and this rushed development programme led to frequent breakdowns and problems with the early Marks. Its size was limited by the British railway loading gauge restrictions, and it suffered from the same disadvantages of other contemporary British designs, namely that it was too narrow to take a larger turret needed for the 17pdr gun. Thus, by 1944–45 it was under-gunned by German standards, although this was offset by heavy armoured protection.

The other factor which made the Churchill one of the most important British tanks of 1939–45 was its adaptability to specialized armour roles (the Funnies) needed for the invasion of Europe in 1944, for example:
• Churchill Oke/Crocodile: flamethrowers.
• Churchill AVRE (Armoured Vehicle, Royal Engineers) Mark I and II: to carry and support assault engineers charged with breaching heavy defences. Fitted with demountable jibs, front and rear, earth spade at rear, and two-speed winch. Also a 290mm/11.42in spigot mortar for demolition tasks.
• Churchill Ark Mark I/II/III: bridge-carrying vehicles able to lay ramps across sea walls or span defence ditches and craters.
• Churchill AMRA (Anti-Mine Roller Attachment)/AMRCR (Anti-Mine Reconnaissance Castor Roller)/CIRD (Canadian Indestructible Roller Device)/Plough/Snake/Conger: mine-clearers using various systems, usually front-mounted to detonate mines.
• Churchill with Bobbin/Twin Bobbins: mat layers for use during beach landings.
• Churchill with mine plough (A–D, Bullshorn/Jeffries and Farmer Ploughs).

ABOVE: **An A22 Infantry Tank Mark IV Churchill. The Churchill Mark I mounted a 2pdr gun and had a 76.2mm/3in howitzer in the hull. From Churchill Mark III onwards its main armament was a 6pdr, and from Mark VIII a 75mm/2.95in gun.**

A22 Infantry Tank Mk IV Churchill (family)

Entered service: 1941
Crew: 5
Weight: Mks III–VI – 39,626kg/39 tons
Mks VII–VIII – 40,642kg/40 tons
Dimensions: Length – 7.44m/24ft 5in
  Height (over turret hatch) – 3.25m/10ft 8in
  Mks VII–VIII – 3.45m/11ft 4in
  Width – 2.74m/9ft
  Mks I–II – 2.49m/8ft 2in
Armament: Main – Mk I – 76.2mm/3in nose-mounted gun and 2pdr turret-mounted gun
  Mks III, IV – 6pdr OQF (ordnance quick-firing) Mk III or V gun
  Mks V, VIII – 95mm/3.74in gun
  Mks VI, VII – 75mm/2.95in L/40 gun
  Secondary – 1 or 2 x 7.92mm/0.312in Besa machine-guns, coaxial or hull-mounted
Armour: Maximum – 102mm/4.02in
  Mks VI–VIII: 152mm/5.98in
Powerplant: Beford 12-cylinder petrol, 261.1kW/350bhp
Performance: Speed – 25kph/15.5mph
  Range – 193km/120 miles

A43 Infantry Tank Black Prince

In December 1943, Allied tanks were still out-gunned and out-armoured by the Germans. Neither the Challenger A30 nor the Sherman Firefly, both of which mounted 17pdr guns, had adequate armoured protection to engage the German Panther and Tiger tanks on equal terms. It was therefore planned to put the 17pdr gun into the more heavily armoured Churchill. The design of the turret was to be governed by the size of the gun – although consideration had still to be given to the possibility of a later even larger calibre gun such as the 94mm/3.7in Mark VI, which had a penetration performance of 25 per cent better than that of the 17pdr.

Owing to the larger turret ring diameter required for the 17pdr gun, the standard Churchill hull was too narrow. An enlarged version was therefore designed, using as many Churchill A22 components as possible, and with the same thickness of armour.

Vauxhall built six pilot models designated A43 and known as Black Prince, with full production scheduled to start by the spring of 1945. Unfortunately, the combination of two other factors caused the project to be shelved. First, the standard 261kW/350hp Bedford engine was found not to be powerful enough for the A43 which weighed 50,802kg/ 50 tons (some 10 tons heavier than the Churchill). Secondly, by the time plans had been made to replace it with the 447.4kW/600hp Rolls-Royce Meteor engine, a decision had been taken to concentrate the future tank programme on one class of tank only, namely the world-beating Centurion, which was on the point of being built.

A43 Infantry Tank Black Prince

Entered service: 1945

Crew: 5

Weight: 50,802kg/50 tons

Dimensions: Length – 8.81m/28ft 11in
   Height (over turret hatch) – 2.74m/9ft
   Width – 3.43m/11ft 3in

Armament: Main – 17pdr gun
   Secondary – 2 x 7.92mm/0.312in Besa
   machine-guns

Armour: Maximum – 152mm/5.98in

Powerplant: Bedford 12-cylinder petrol,
   261kW/350hp

Performance: Speed – 18kph/11mph
   Range – 161km/100 miles

BELOW: **The A43 Infantry Tank Black Prince or Super Churchill. It mounted a 17pdr gun, which required the redesign and widening of the hull. Six prototypes were built. However, the A41 Centurion proved to be a far superior tank, and Black Prince was scrapped.**

A24 Cruiser Tank Mark VII Cavalier

LEFT: The A24 Cruiser Tank Mark VII Cavalier was requested in late 1940 to overcome all the problems inherent in the earlier cruisers. Fitted with a Mark III or Mark V 6pdr gun, the latter was distinguishable from the prominent counterweight on the muzzle.

A24 Cruiser Tank Mk VII Cavalier

Entered service: 1941
Crew: 5
Weight: 26,925kg/26.5 tons
Dimensions: Length – 6.35m/20ft 10in
Height (over turret hatch) – 2.44m/8ft
Width –2.9m/9ft 6in
Armament: Main – 6pdr OQF (ordnance quick-firing) gun
Secondary – 1 or 2 x 7.92mm/0.312in Besa machine-guns
Armour: Maximum – 76mm/2.99in
Powerplant: Nuffield Liberty V12 petrol, 253.64kW/340bhp
Performance: Speed –39kph/24mph
Range – 266km/165 miles

Experience with Crusader and its predecessors in World War II led to the production of the first new wartime Cruiser, the Cavalier, which had thicker armour, a bigger gun (the 6pdr) and wider tracks. All this increased its weight by over an extra 5,080kg/5 tons more than the Crusader and consequently reduced its top speed because it used the same engine and power train despite improvements in its suspension.

Externally it was almost identical in appearance to both the Cromwell and Centaur. The Cavalier was only built in small numbers and was never used operationally as a gun tank. Some had the 6pdr gun replaced with a dummy barrel and were used for artillery OP (Observation Post), while others were converted to an ARV (Armoured Recovery Vehicle) role with the turret removed and a winch and a demountable A-frame jib fitted.

A27L Cruiser Tank Mark VIII Centaur

LEFT: The A27L Cruiser Tank Mark VIII Centaur. Like the Cavalier, it too was initially called Cromwell, but changed to Centaur. Nearly 1,000 were built, with 80 mounting the 95mm/3.74in close-support howitzer instead of the 6pdr gun.

A27L Cruiser Tank Mk VIII Centaur

Entered service: 1942
Crew: 5
Weight: 28,849kg/28.4 tons
Dimensions: Length – 6.35m/20ft 10in
Height (over turret hatch) – 2.49m/8ft 2in
Width – 2.9m/9ft 6in
Armament: Main – Mk I – 6pdr OQF (ordnance quick-firing) gun
Mk IV – 95mm/3.74in howitzer
Secondary – 1 or 2 x 7.92mm/0.312in Besa machine-guns
Armour: Maximum – 76mm/2.99in
Powerplant: Nuffield Liberty V12 petrol
Performance: Speed – 43.5kph/27mph
Range – 266km/165 miles

Next in the Cruiser line was the A27L Centaur, which was unfortunately compromised from the start by production shortages. The intention was to fit this tank with a new powerful Rolls-Royce Meteor engine. However, supplies were not available because all production was required for aircraft. Consequently the old Liberty V12 engine was fitted instead. Some Centaurs were later upgraded to Cromwells (the Mark X) with a Meteor engine retro-fit, while

others had their existing engines up-rated, and were armed with a 95mm/3.74in howitzer to be used by the Royal Marines to give supporting fire from LCTs (Landing Craft Tanks) during the D-Day landings. A few were also converted for special-purpose roles, including AA (Anti-Aircraft) tanks, ARVs (Armoured Recovery Vehicles), OP (Observation Post) vehicles, and Dozers, all being used in the 1944–45 north-west Europe campaign.

A27M Cruiser Tank Mark VIII Cromwell

Early Cromwells closely resembled the Cavalier and Centaur, except, of course, for the fitting of the Meteor engine – hence the letter "M" in their title. The Meteor engine was a 447.4kW/ 600hp V12, and made Cromwell the fastest Cruiser tank so far, with increased reliability. It went on to become the most used British cruiser tank of World War II, and formed the main equipment of British armoured divisions from 1944–45, together with the US-built Sherman M4.

Cromwell's hull and turret were of simple box shape and its construction composite – an inner skin with an outer layer of armour bolted on. An important difference between early and later models was the introduction of all-welded construction process in place of riveting, which further simplified the mass production of the vehicle.

ABOVE: **An excellent photograph of an A27M Cruiser Tank Mark VIII Cromwell. Light, fast and armed with a 75mm/2.95in gun, initially it did not do well in Normandy but came into its own when the battle became more fluid.** BELOW: **A cutaway drawing of the Cromwell showing its main components, with the engine and transmission at the rear.**

Undoubtedly there were misgivings among many tank crews when they were converted from Sherman to Cromwell (the 7th Armoured Division was re-equipped with Cromwells when they returned to the UK from Italy to prepare for D-Day) because of its lack of firepower – it was armed with either a 75mm/2.95in or a 6pdr gun, neither of which was a real match for the German Tiger and Panther tanks. The narrowness of the Cromwell's hull prevented it from being further up-gunned until an

extensive redesign had been implemented, and it was not until after the end of World War II that this took place. Here is how one experienced 7th Armoured Division tank crewman summed up the Cromwell: "I think it was a useless tank – fast enough – but without adequate armour and under-gunned." To be fair, however, once the Normandy "bocage" country was left behind and speed became more important than tank versus tank battles, then the Cromwell did far better, although its basic faults remained.

The design was also flexible enough to be fitted with wider tracks and employed in specialist roles. These included:
• Cromwell ARV (Armoured Recovery Vehicle): vehicle with turret removed and winch and demountable A-frame jib fitted.
• Cromwell Command/OP (Observation Post): fitted with dummy gun and extra radio equipment.
• Cromwell CIRD (Canadian Indestructible Roller Device): vehicle fitted with CIRD mine-exploder.
• Cromwell Prong: standard vehicle fitted with Culin Hedgerow Cutting Device fitted to cut through "bocage" hedgerows.

A27M Cruiser Tank Mk VIII Cromwell

Entered service: 1943
Crew: 5
Weight: 27,941kg/27.5 tons
Dimensions: Length – 6.35m/20ft 10in
  Height (over turret hatch) – 2.49m/8ft 2in
  Width – 2.9m/9ft 6in
Armament: Main – Mk I–III – 6pdr gun
  Mks IV, V, VII 75mm/2.95in OQF (ordnance quick-firing) gun
  Mks VI, VII – 95mm/3.74in howitzer
  Secondary – 1 or 2 x 7.92mm/0.312in Besa machine-guns (one coaxial, one hull-mounted)
Armour: Maximum – 76mm/2.99in (101mm/3.98in with appliqué)
Powerplant: Rolls-Royce Meteor V12 petrol
Performance: Speed – Mk I–III – 64.4kph/40mph
  Mk IVs on – 52kph/32mph
  Range – 278km/173 miles

A34 Cruiser Tank Comet

The next logical development of the Centaur/Cromwell design was to produce a tank that really had the firepower, protection and mobility to match its German counterparts. This was to be the Comet, which, like the last Marks of Cromwell, was of an all-welded construction and at 35,560kg/ 35 tons was nearly 5,080kg/5 tons heavier than the last up-armoured version of the Cromwell series. It was to all intents and purposes an up-gunned, up-armoured Cromwell, retaining many similar features and components, as well as the same general layout. The initial Comet prototype was the last British cruiser to have the Christie suspension (the same as the Cromwell but with the top rollers) and it had a good cross-country performance and a top speed of 47kph/29mph.

Where it departed from its predecessor was in mounting a completely redesigned main gun, a 76.2mm/3in, known as the 77mm, which had just about the same performance as the 17pdr, but was smaller and lighter.

TOP: **Undoubtedly the best British tank of the war was the A34 Cruiser Tank Comet. Bearing the Black Bull divisional sign of 11th Armoured Division, this one was photographed at Bovington, Dorset. Comet was not available in sufficient numbers until after the Rhine Crossing in March 1945.** ABOVE: **Comets of the 1st Royal Tank Regiment on parade in Berlin, September 20, 1945, when they were inspected by Field Marshal Montgomery.**

Fast and reliable, the Comet was the best all-round British tank produced during World War II, but was introduced far too late to have much effect on tank versus tank combat. Production deliveries started late in 1944, but regiments did not receive issues until after the Rhine Crossing in March 1945. Fast and reliable, it was the first British tank to begin to match the German PzKpfw V Panther in all-round performance,

especially firepower. It would remain in service for the next 15 years, the last Comets not being withdrawn from British service until 1960. Its successor was the A41 Centurion.

Visually, Comet is quickly distinguishable from Cromwell by virtue of the four return rollers above the road wheels. Note also the prominent commander's all-round vision cupola, the forward-sloping turret roof and the large counterweight on the turret rear.

Comet was thus the last British tank to be developed during World War II and the last in the cruiser line, as its successor the A41 Centurion was classed as the first "universal" tank. Initially there was some criticism of Comet concerning the retention of the hull gunner and the thinness of the belly armour, as mines became more and more of a threat during the later stages of the campaigns of north-west Europe. However, these faults were deliberately ignored in order to get it into operational service.

A34 Cruiser Tank Comet

Entered service: 1945

Crew: 5

Weight: 35,560kg/35 tons

Dimensions: Length – 7.66m/25ft 1.5in
Height (over turret hatch) – 2.68m/8ft 9.5in
Width – 3.05m/10ft

Armament: Main – 77mm (76.2mm/3in) OQF (ordnance quick-firing) gun
Secondary – 2 x 7.92mm/0.312in Besa machine-guns (one coaxial and one hull-mounted)

Armour: Maximum – 101mm/3.98in

Powerplant: Rolls-Royce Meteor V12 petrol, 447.4kW/600bhp

Performance: Speed – 47kph/29mph
Range – 198km/123 miles

TOP: **Ready for battle! A Comet tank "bombed up" and ready for action.**

ABOVE LEFT AND ABOVE: **Views of the Comet during the war. Comet remained in British Army service for many years after the end of World War II. It was also in service with the Irish Army from 1950–70. It was the "end of the line" for British cruiser tanks, which had begun with the A9 and A10 in the early 1930s.**

LEFT: The massive A39 Heavy Assault Tank Tortoise. Six pilot models were built from August 1945 onwards but were not trialled until 1946–47.

A39 Heavy Assault Tank Tortoise

Entered service: 1946–47 (pilot models only)
Crew: 7
Weight: 79,252kg/78 tons
Dimensions: Length – 10.06m/33ft
　　Height (over turret hatch) – 3.05m/10ft
　　Width – 3.91m/12ft 10in
Armament: Main – 32pdr OQF (ordnance quick-firing) gun
　　Secondary – 3 x Besa 7.92mm/0.312in machine-guns, 2 in AA (anti-aircraft) mount
Armour: Maximum – 225mm/8.86in
Powerplant: Rolls-Royce Meteor V12 petrol, 484.7kW/650bhp
Performance: Speed – 19kph/12mph
　　Range – 81km/50 miles

A39 Heavy Assault Tank Tortoise

The last of the British attempts to produce a heavy tank during World War II was the equivalent of the Jagdtiger, a 79,252kg/78-ton monster, appropriately called Tortoise. With a 32pdr main gun having limited traverse, it had armour up to 225mm/8.86in thick and a crew of seven. Although it was first designed in 1942, work progressed slowly until 1944, when the Jagdtiger appeared and the project received extra impetus; however, the pilot models were not delivered until after the war had ended. In trials, performance and manoeuvrability were adequate, with a top speed of 19kph/12mph, but ultimately Tortoise was really too heavy to be a feasible proposition.

TOG 1 and TOG 2 Heavy Tanks

LEFT: TOG 2 after restoration. The massive tank then mounted a 17pdr gun in the large turret that would later be fitted to the A30 Challenger.

TOG Heavy Tank

Entered service: 1940 (prototypes only)
Crew: TOG 1 – 6; TOG 2 – 8
Weight: TOG 1 – 64,555kg/63.5 tons
　　TOG 2 – 81,284kg/80 tons
Dimensions: Length – 10.13m/33ft 3in
　　Height (over turret hatch) – 3.05m/10ft
　　Width – 3.12m/10ft 3in
Armament: Main – TOG 1 – 2pdr in turret and a 75mm/2.95in howitzer in nose
　　TOG 2 – 6pdr (77mm/3.03in) or 17pdr OQF (ordnance quick-firing) gun
　　Secondary – None fitted
Armour: Maximum – 75mm/2.95in
Powerplant: Paxman-Ricardo V12 diesel, 447.4kW/600bhp
Performance: Speed – 14kph/8.5mph
　　Range – 81km/50 miles

The acronym TOG stands for "The Old Gang" and refers to the team set up on the outbreak of World War II to find solutions to UK tank needs. The members were all men who had been directly responsible for the very successful World War I tank programme: Stern, Wilson, Swinton, d'Eyncourt, Ricardo, Symes and Tritton. They now produced a very large, heavy tank, weighing some 81,284kg/80 tons, which was long enough to cross wide trenches and well protected against anti-tank weapons. TOG 1 had a 75mm/2.95in howitzer in its nose and a 2pdr in a Matilda II-type turret above, and would probably have been ideal to fight the largely static battles of World War I but was entirely wrong for the Blitzkrieg of World War II.

The trials of TOG 1 revealed problems with the electric transmission, and so a hydraulic transmission was tried out on TOG 2, which also mounted a larger turret and a 6pdr gun (later changed to a 17pdr). This was the heaviest British tank of World War II; however, during development the Churchill was produced, trialled and accepted, so interest in TOG waned. It became yet another failed design project, and TOG 2 (Revised) was never built.

BT Medium Tank series

This series of Soviet medium tanks owes its existence to the purchase of an American M1931 Christie tank by the Soviet Purchasing Commission. It had, like the original Christie tank, the ability to run either on its tracks or on its road wheels (four large road wheels on each side). The Soviets did their copying very thoroughly and the BT-1 was made to the same all-riveted construction as the American M1931, with a similar turret containing two machine-guns. Even the engine was a copy of the Liberty from the Christie model.

The BT-1 was only a limited production run, soon replaced by the BT-2 which had a new turret mounting a 37mm/1.46in gun and a machine-gun. This was the first major production model and weighed about a ton more than its predecessor.

The next model was the BT-3/BT-4, again very similar but with solid disc wheels rather than spoked wheels. It also had a 45mm/1.77in gun as its main armament. Production was limited, but there were conversion models: one (in 1939) which had a new turret mounting a flamethrower, while another had its gun removed and carried a folding wooden bridge – neither went into full production.

Then came the major production model, the BT-5, with a larger cylindrical turret mounting a 45mm/1.77in gun and coaxial machine-gun, better vision devices, a strengthened suspension and a new, more powerful engine. The BT-5A model was for close-support work and mounted a 76.2mm/3in howitzer instead of the 45mm/1.77in gun. There was also a command version which had an extensive frame aerial around the turret and a radio inside at the rear.

Next in line was the BT-7 which had a new conical turret (with a ball-mounted machine-gun in its rear) on all except the earliest vehicles. It was of an all-welded construction, with a new, more powerful engine, a new gearbox, more space for extra fuel and ammunition stowage and thicker frontal armour. This model was the main type in service from the beginning of World War II until the end of 1941. Like its predecessor, there was also both a close-support version (76.2mm/3in howitzer) and a command version (BT-7-1 (V)).

Drastic redesign then took place, the BT-7M model being considerably more streamlined with more room for the new V2 diesel engine, sloped front glacis plate rather than the distinctive "V" nose and the same turret as the T-28 medium tank. It was also known as the BT-8.

Final development was the BT-IS, which was only built as a prototype, but was significantly different in design, being the first Red Army tank to have sloping side armour and front glacis.

ABOVE AND LEFT: **The BT-7 Red Army Medium Tank was the direct descendant of the BT heritage that owes its origin to the Christie M1931 from which it was copied. All had the pointed front glacis and large roadwheels, which gave them high cross-country speed. Heavier than the BT-5, it had an improved conical turret, mounting a 45mm/1.77in gun and was the main tank in Russian service during 1940–41.**

BT Medium Tank series (1, 2, 5 and 7) family

	BT-1	BT-2	BT-5	BT-7
Entered service:	1932	1933	1935	1936
Crew: 3				
Weight: kg	10,200	11,200	11,500	13,900
tons	10	11	11.3	13.7
Dimensions:				
Length m	5.49	5.49	5.49	5.66
ft in	18	18	18	18 / 7
Height m	1.93	1.93	2.21	2.41
ft in	6 / 4	6 / 4	7 / 3	7 / 11
Width m	2.24	2.24	2.24	2.43
ft in	7 / 4	7 / 4	7 / 4	7 / 11.5

Armament: Main – BT-1 – 2 x machine-guns; BT-2 – 1 x 37mm/1.46in gun; BT-5 and BT-7 – 1 x 45mm/1.77in gun

Secondary – All 1 x 7.62mm/0.3in DT machine-gun, except BT-7 2 x 7.62mm/0.3in DT machine-guns

Armour: Maximum – All 13mm/0.5in, except BT-7 – 22mm/0.87in

Powerplant: All Liberty Aero V12 petrol, 298.5kW/400bhp, except BT-7 – M-15T V12 petrol, 335.8kW/450bhp

Performance:

Speed tracks – All 65kph/40mph, except BT-7 – 72kph/45mph

Speed wheels – BT-1/2 – 105kph/65mph; BT-5 – 112kph/70mph

Range tracks – All c200km/124 miles, except BT-7 – c400km/249 miles

Range wheels – All c300km/186 miles, except BT-7 – c500km/311 miles

Carro Armato M11/39 Medium Tank

LEFT: The M11/39 Medium Tank directly evolved from the Carro Armato tank of 1935. A hundred were ordered following the Spanish Civil War which had revealed inadequacies in the small CV33 and CV35 tankettes. They proved to be no match for the British tanks in the early days of the desert war.

Carro Armato M11/39 Medium Tank

Entered service: 1939
Crew: 3
Weight: 11,000kg/10.8 tons
Dimensions: Length – 4.74m/15ft 6.5in
 Height (over turret hatch) – 2.3m/7ft 6.5in
 Width – 2.21m/7ft 3in
Armament: Main – 37mm/1.46in Vickers-Terni L/40 gun
 Secondary – 2 x 8mm/0.315in Breda Model 38 machine-guns
Armour: Maximum – 30mm/1.18in
Powerplant: Fiat SPA 8T V8 diesel, 78.3kW/105bhp
Performance: Speed – 32kph/20mph
 Range – 200km/124 miles

At almost 11 tons, this was the start of the Italian medium tank line and evolved from lighter versions. The main armament was a 37mm/1.46in hull-mounted gun, while the manually operated turret, offset to the left, contained twin 8mm/0.315in Breda machine-guns. Although it had an adequate diesel engine and a good sprung bogie suspension, its riveted armour was very thin, giving minimal protection to its crew, so it was of very little use in battle and fell as easy prey to the British tanks when it went into action in Libya in 1940. Many were knocked out, while a few were captured and used by the Australians in the North African desert in early 1941. The M11/39 was soon withdrawn from service.

Carro Armato M13/40 Medium Tank

Developed in 1939, this tank was largely based upon the M11/39, although at almost 14 tons it was larger and had slightly thicker armour. Its main armament was a new high-velocity 47mm/1.85in gun and coaxial 8mm/0.315in Breda machine-gun, which was mounted in the turret, replacing the twin 8mm/ 0.315in Breda machine-guns which were now gimbal-mounted in the front hull.

It was probably the best and most widely used Italian tank of World War II, although it was still no match for its opponents. Initially in the desert it suffered from mechanical failure and had to be tropicalized (especially against the sand which got into everything mechanical), with the fitting of improved air and fuel filters. The M13/40 saw action during the first campaign in the North African desert, and despite its excellent gun, it soon proved easy meat for the British heavy infantry tanks

LEFT: Probably the most widely used Italian tank of the war, the M13/40 was still no match for the British Matilda II. It first saw action in December 1940 in Libya, but its armoured protection proved inadequate in battle, even in 1940. This one is at the Aberdeen Proving Ground in the USA.

Carro Armato M13/40 Medium Tank

Entered service: 1940
Crew: 4
Weight: 14,000kg/13.8 tons
Dimensions: Length – 4.90m/16ft 1in
 Height (over turret hatch) – 2.39m/7ft 10in
 Width – 2.21m/7ft 3in
Armament: Main – 47mm/1.85in Model 37 L/32 Ansaldo gun
 Secondary – 3 x 8mm/0.315in Breda Model 38 machine-guns (one coaxial and two hull-mounted)
Armour: Maximum – 42mm/1.65in
Powerplant: SPA 8 TM40 V8 diesel, 93kW/125bhp
Performance: Speed – 32kph/20mph
 Range – 200km/124 miles

(Matilda II). During the resounding defeat of the 10th Italian Army at Beda Fomm/ Sidi Saleh, Libya, in February 1941, over a hundred M13/40s were captured in pristine condition. These were used to equip both the British 6th Royal Tank Regiment and the Australian 6th Cavalry as a temporary, emergency measure.

Carro Veloce 33 Tankette

In 1929 the Italians purchased some Vickers Carden-Loyd Mark VI tankettes from Britain, and at the same time obtained permission to manufacture them in Italy. A total of 25 were built under the designation Carro Veloce 29 by Ansaldo, with automotive parts from Fiat. The CV33 was directly descended from the CV29, designed and built by Ansaldo from 1931–32. There were various models over the years of this little two-man tankette. The usual armament was either one or two Breda machine-guns; however, from 1940 some vehicles were re-armed with a 20mm/0.79in Solothurn anti-tank gun while all had a stronger suspension, new tracks and better vision devices for the driver.

LEFT: **The Carro Veloce 33 – this is an early production model – was armed with either a single 6.5mm/0.256in machine-gun or twin 8mm/0.315in machine-guns. A mass of these little tankettes looked most impressive but were no real use even against light tanks with thicker armour and bigger guns.**

Carro Veloce 33 Tankette

Entered service: 1933
Crew: 2
Weight: 3,200kg/3.2 tons
Dimensions: Length – 3.18m/10ft 5in
　　Height (over turret hatch) – 1.3m/4ft 3in
　　Width – 1.42m/4ft 8in
Armament: Main – 1 x 6.5mm/0.26in or
　　2 x 8mm/0.32in Breda machine-guns
Armour: Maximum – 14mm/0.55in
Powerplant: FIAT-SPA CV3 4-cylinder petrol,
　　31kW/42bhp
Performance: Speed – 42kph/26mph
　　Range – 125km/78 miles

Carro Veloce L35/Lf Flamethrower Tankette

LEFT: **The flamethrowing version of the small Italian tankette was the L35/Lf, which towed a trailer full of flame fluid (later models had the fuel tank mounted in the rear of the tankette above the engine). This model is on show at the Bovington Tank Museum, Dorset. Other L35s were fitted with eight bridges: L3/35(P) – *Passarella* (Gangway).**

Carro Veloce L35/Lf Flamethrower Tankette

Entered service: 1933
Crew: 2
Weight: 3,200kg/3.2 tons
Dimensions: Length – 3.18m/10ft 5in
　　Height (over turret hatch) – 1.3m/4ft 3in
　　Width – 1.42m/4ft 8in
Armament: Main – Lanciaflamme Flamethrower
Armour: Maximum – 14mm/0.55in
Powerplant: FIAT-SPA CV3 4-cylinder petrol,
　　31kW/42bhp
Performance: Speed – 42kph/26mph
　　Range – 125km/78 miles

The Carro Veloce L35/Lf (*Lanciaflamme*) was the flamethrower variant of the CV33 tankette. It had a long-barrelled hooded flamethrower instead of the usual machine-guns. A 500-litre/110-gallon armoured fuel trailer was towed behind the *carro d'assalto lanciafiamme*. On a later model the flamethrower fuel tank was mounted on the rear of the vehicle. The range of the flamethrower was about 100m/328ft.

Char d'Assault Schneider CA1 Heavy Tank

Char d'Assault Schneider CA1 Heavy Tank	
Entered service: 1916	
Crew: 7	
Weight: 12,500kg/12.3 tons	
Dimensions: Length – 6.32m/20ft 8in	
Height (over turret hatch) – 2.3m/7ft 6in	
Width – 2.05m/6ft 9in	
Armament: Main – 75mm/2.95in gun	
Secondary – 2 x 8mm/0.315in Hotchkiss machine-guns	
Armour: Maximum – 11mm/0.43in	
Powerplant: Schneider, 4-cylinder petrol, 41kW/55bhp	
Performance: Speed – 8.1kph/5mph	
Range – 80km/49.7 miles	

LEFT: **The Schneider CA1 was the first French tank to be designed in World War I. The first of the 400 to be built were delivered in September 1916, not long after the first British tanks made their appearance. It had vertically coiled spring suspension.**

The Schneider CA1 was the first French tank to be designed and, as with many designs of the time, it was based upon the Holt tractor chassis. The first of those built was delivered in September 1916, so the French were not very far behind the British in the design and production of this new type of weapon system. The driving force was Colonel (later General) Jean Baptiste Estienne, who is reputed to have said, "Whoever shall first be able to make land ironclads armed and equipped ... will have won the war." Designed by Eugene Brille of the Schneider Company, the Char d'Assault Schneider CA1 weighed 12,500kg/12.3 tons, mounted a 75mm/2.95in gun in a sponson on the right-hand side of the tank along with two 8mm/0.315in machine-guns, one on each side. It had a crew of seven men and rear main access doors. Note also the nosepiece which acted as a wire-cutter, important for cutting barbed wire.

RIGHT: **On the left side the sponson just contained a machine-gun. This is a late-production CA1 with improved roof ventilation and larger fuel tanks.**

The Schneider was first committed to battle at Berry-au-Bac on April 16, 1917. 132 Schneider's in eight companies were organized into two columns and reached their objectives but were then subjected to heavy enemy fire and many were lost – 76 in total – with 57 being completely destroyed by artillery. The other main reason for such heavy losses was the

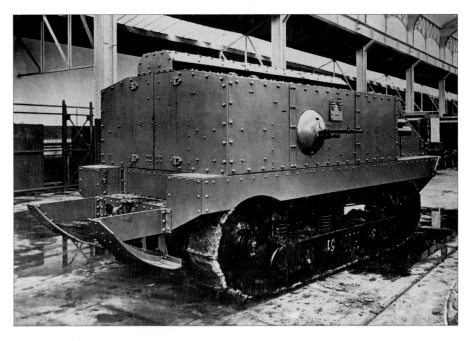

vulnerability of the Schneider's fuel tanks to the German "K" anti-tank bullet.

Late production models attempted to solve these problems with better-protected fuel tanks and more roof ventilation than the earlier model.

Schneider also built a prototype CA2 with a turret-mounted 47mm/1.85in main gun, but this was never put into production.

Char d'Assault Saint Chamond Heavy Tank

The second French heavy tank of World War I was the Saint Chamond, designed by a Colonel Rimailho and built in 1916 by the *Compagnie des Forges et Acieries de la Marine et d'Homércourt*, whose factory at Saint Chamond gave the tank its name. At almost 23 tons, it was heavier than the Schneider, had a large crew of nine, mounted a 75mm/2.95in gun in its nose, and also had four machine-guns, positioned two to each side of the vehicle. It was easily identified from its front hull and flat roof.

ABOVE: **Some 400 Saint Chamonds were built in 1916.** BELOW: **On later models of the St Chamond, the original gun was replaced by a regular Model 1897 field gun.**

The Saint Chamond had an electric transmission, with a 67.1kW/90bhp Panhard motor driving a dynamo which powered two electric motors – one per track, with a top speed of 12kph/7.45mph. Despite this, its cross-country performance was indifferent, as it tended to bury its nose when negotiating soft going.

By mid-range production of the vehicle, the two cylindrical cupolas were replaced by a flat pitched roof. Later models reinstalled a single, flat-topped cupola on the right for the driver, and replaced the original main gun with the regular 75mm/2.95in Model 1897 field gun.

A total of 400 Saint Chamonds were built, and the tank first saw action in early May 1917, but the design problem with the nose was insurmountable and the quest for a perfect heavy tank moved on.

Char d'Assault Saint Chamond Heavy Tank

Entered service: 1917
Crew: 9
Weight: 23,000kg/22.64 tons
Dimensions: Length – 8.83m/28ft 11.5in
    Height (over turret hatch) – 2.36m/7ft 9in
    Width – 2.67m/8ft 9in
Armament: Main – 75mm/2.95in 1897 Model
    field gun
    Secondary – 4 x 8mm/0.315in Hotchkiss
    machine-guns
Armour: Maximum – 17mm/0.67in
Powerplant: Panhard, 4-cylinder petrol
    67.1kW/90bhp
Performance: Speed – 12kph/7.45mph
    Range – 60km/37.3 miles

LEFT: **Coming into service in 1935, with 40mm/1.57in of armour plate and a 75mm/2.95in gun in its belly, the Char B1 was one of the most formidable tanks in the world at that time. The Char B1-bis was even heavier, with a larger secondary armament in its turret and thicker armour. This Char B1 is on parade in Paris in 1936.**

Char B1 Heavy Tank

Entered service: 1931
Crew: 4
Weight: 30,480kg /30 tons
Dimensions: Length – 6.37m/20ft 11in
Height (over turret hatch) – 2.82m/9ft 3in
Width – 2.49m/8ft 2in
Armament: Main – 1 x 75mm/2.95in short gun in hull and 1 x 47mm/1.85in gun in turret
Secondary – 2 x 7.5mm/0.295in machine-guns (one in hull, one in turret)
Armour: Maximum – 40mm/1.57in
Powerplant: Renault, 6-cylinder petrol, 134.2kW/180bhp
Performance: Speed – 28kph/17.4mph
Range – 150km/93 miles

Char B1 Heavy Tank

The development of the Renault Char de Bataille B1 began in the 1920s when, at the request of General Estienne ("Father of the French Tank Corps"), a consortium of French companies designed a new tank under the codename *Tracteur 30*, with specifications for a vehicle with high mobility and heavy fire power. The result was the Char B1, a tank with considerable potential.

Armed with a short 75mm/2.95in gun carried in a front hull mounting, the sighting of the weapon was controlled by the driver, and corrections were made by moving the tank. The sophisticated Naeder Steering Unit, which allowed delicate and very accurate adjustment, had a double differential and hydrostatic drive, which gave the "infinitely variable steering" necessary to lay the 75mm/

2.95in gun. There was also a fixed 7.5mm/0.295in machine-gun controlled by the driver, both weapons being loaded by a crewman sitting beside him. In the turret there was a coaxially mounted 47mm/1.85in anti-tank gun and 7.5mm/0.295in machine-gun fired by the commander. This gun layout effectively halved the amount of ammunition the vehicle could carry.

Char B1-bis Heavy Tank

Char B1-bis Heavy Tank

Entered service: 1935
Crew: 4
Weight: 32,500kg/32 tons
Dimensions: Length – 6.52m/21ft 5in
Height (over turret hatch) – 2.79m/9ft 2in
Width – 2.5m/8ft 2in
Armament: Main – 1 x 75mm/2.95in short gun in hull and 1 x 47mm/1.85in gun in turret
Secondary – 2 x 7.5mm/0.295in machine-guns
Armour: Maximum – 60mm/2.36in
Powerplant: Renault, 6-cylinder petrol, 223.7kW/300bhp
Performance: Speed – 28kph/17.4mph
Range – 180km/111.8 miles

The B1-bis version evolved from the B1 and appeared in 1935. It had thicker armour, a larger gun in the turret (47mm/1.85in instead of 37mm/1.46in) and a more powerful 223.7kW/300bhp Renault aircraft engine. Again no traverse was possible for its nose-mounted 75mm/

ABOVE: **A Char B1-bis (Encore). Note the new AP x 4 turret and 47mm/1.85in gun.**

2.95in gun, so to lay in azimuth the tank had to be turned on its tracks. Of the 365 Char B1-bis built, large numbers were captured in a serviceable condition by

the Germans in France in 1940. Although one of the best armed and armoured tanks of its day, these captured B1s were not immediately issued to German fighting units, because of the limitations of the one-man turret and the tank's generally poor performance. Instead they were used as training vehicles or fitted with radio sets and used to equip second line units, mainly in the west.

Char 2C Heavy Tank

During World War I, the French had issued a specification for a heavy "breakthrough" tank, Char de Rupture C, at a weight of about 40 tons. Two prototypes, Chars 1A and 1B were produced from 1917–18. Further development then produced an even heavier tank of nearly 70 tons – and this was the Char 2C. Although it did not become operational during the war, ten were built, the last being delivered in 1922. In their day they were the most powerful tanks in the world, with a crew of twelve, a 75mm/2.95in gun in the front turret and four machine-guns (one in an auxiliary turret at the rear of the tank). One of them was converted to mount a 155mm/6.1in howitzer as well as the 75mm/2.95in gun and the four machine-guns, and this led some Intelligence circles to think that France was building large numbers of "super tanks". The Char 2C had two engines totalling 186.4kW/250bhp, driving electric generators to run a motor for each track, giving the tank a top speed of 12kph/7.5mph.

The last of these tanks were destroyed in 1940 by enemy air attack or captured, when they were being transported to the front by train.

TOP: **Ten Char 2C Heavy Tanks were produced before the end of the war in 1918, but did not see operational service until 1921. They were fitted with German engines provided as part of post-war reparations.** ABOVE: **The massive Char 2C Heavy Tank was designed by FCM and was selected as the "breakthrough" tank for the large scale offensive planned for 1919, but was never needed.** BELOW LEFT: **In 1940, the surviving six Char 2Cs were destroyed or captured by the Germans while still on railway flat cars. The 2C had a crew of 12 men. Here, one still on its flat car is under German guard.**

Char 2C Heavy Tank

Entered service: 1918
Crew: 12
Weight: 69,000kg/67.9 tons
Dimensions: Length – 10.26m/33ft 8in
Height (over turret hatch) – 4m/13ft 1in
Width – 2.95m/9ft 8in
Armament: Main – 75mm/2.95in
Secondary – 4 x 8mm/0.315in Hotchkiss machine-guns
Armour: Maximum – 45mm/1.77in
Powerplant: 2 x Daimler or Maybach, 6-cylinder petrol, 387.7kW/520bhp
Performance: Speed – 12kph/7.5mph
Range – 100km/62.1 miles

Elefant/Ferdinand Heavy Tank Destroyer

This 65,000kg/64-ton tank destroyer/ heavy assault gun mounted an 8.8cm/3.46in StuK 43/2 L/71 gun in a limited traverse mount. The monstrous Ferdinand (named in honour of its creator Ferdinand Porsche) was ideal when used as a long-range tank killer, but not nearly as effective as an assault gun because of its lack of traverse and the absence of any close-in defensive capability. At Kursk its performance was disappointing, and almost all were lost to determined Soviet tank-killer teams.

This problem was solved to a degree with the fitting of an MG34 (*Maschinengewehr 34*), but Elefant was really only at its best when fighting at long range – it is reputed to have knocked out a T-34 at a distance of 4.82km/3 miles. Another improvement to the superstructure of about half the Elefants built was the fitting of a cupola for the commander.

Elefant/Ferdinand Heavy TD	
Entered service: 1942	
Crew: 6	
Weight: 65,000kg/64 tons	
Dimensions: Length – 8.14m/26ft 8in	
Height (over turret hatch) – 2.97m/9ft 9in	
Width – 3.38m/11ft 1in	
Armament: Main – 8.8cm/3.46in gun	
Secondary – 7.92mm/0.312in machine-gun	
Armour: Maximum – 200mm/7.87in	
Powerplant: 2 x Maybach HL120TRM V12 petrol, each developing 223.7kW/300bhp	
Performance: Speed – 30kph/18.6mph	
Range – 150km/93.2 miles	

LEFT: **The *Sturmgeschutz mit 8.8cm(3.46in) PaK43/2 (Sd Kfz 184),* to give its full title, was a heavy assault gun/tank destroyer, known as both Elefant and Ferdinand (the latter in honour of Dr Ferdinand Porsche). Only 90 of these massive vehicles were produced, and they first fought at Kursk, from July to August 1943.**

Jagdpanzer IV Tank Destroyer

The PzKpfw IV chassis was used for a number of excellent tank destroyers, over 3,500 being produced and used to great effect in battle. The first Jagdpanzer IV replaced the StuG III in early 1944, weighing nearly 24 tons; with a 7.5cm/ 2.95in PaK39 L/48 gun and carrying 79 rounds, it was basically an improved version of its predecessor. The next development Jagdpanzer IV/70(V) and Jagdpanzer IV/70(A) followed later in the year, mounting the deadly new Vomag long-barrelled 7.5cm/2.95in PaK42 L/70 main gun, with a performance similar to that of Panther. The only difference between these two new Marks was the manufacturer – "V" for Vomag and "A" for Alkett.

Jagdpanzer IV TD	
Entered service: 1943	
Crew: 4	
Weight: 24,000kg/23.6 tons	
Dimensions: Length – 6.85m/22ft 6in	
Height (over turret hatch) – 1.85m/6ft 1in	
Width – 3.17m/10ft 5in	
Armament: Main – 7.5cm/2.95in gun	
Secondary – 1 or 2 x 7.92mm/0.312in machine-guns	
Armour: Maximum – 100mm/3.94in	
Powerplant: Maybach HL120TRM, V12 petrol, 522kW/700hp	
Performance: Speed – 40kph/24.9mph	
Range – 210km/130.5 miles	

LEFT: **The Panzer IV/70(V) (*Sd Kfz 162/1*) was another German tank destroyer. It was an improved version of the Jagdpanzer IV which itself had been an improved version of the StuG III. This one is at the Aberdeen Proving Ground in the USA.**

E-100 Super Heavy Tank

In May 1945 at the Henschel tank proving ground and development centre near Kassel, an enormous experimental heavy tank was discovered by the Allied forces. It weighed approximately 138 tons, with its external features resembling the Tiger Model B tank, but with increased length and width, heavier armour plate, wider tracks and a new suspension system.

The E-100 heavy tank that the Allies had found was the most advanced of an entirely new series of tanks which the German weapons procurement department had initiated in mid-1943. Known as the E-Series, its purpose

was ultimately to replace all the current tanks with a new group of standardized vehicles (E-10, E-25, E-50, E-100), incorporating all the improvements learned from five years AFV combat. However, by the end of the war only this prototype vehicle had been built.

The E-100 was to have been armed with the same weapons as Maus in the same Krupp turret, although one was never fitted. The tank was to have been powered by a Maybach 12-cylinder "V" type engine, developing 521.9kW/700hp, though for initial testing a normal Tiger B H1 230 P30 engine was fitted. With tracks nearly 102cm/40in wide, the

E-100 had a ground pressure of nearly 1.4kg/cm^2 (20psi), while its suspension comprised a series of overlapping steel road wheels, with MAN disc springs – so it did indeed look very like the Tiger B.

In fact, the E-100, like the Maus, was an absurd "wonder weapon" dreamed up to keep an insane Führer happy. It was doomed from the start by its weight.

E-100 Super Heavy Tank

Entered service: 1945 (prototype only)
Crew: 5
Weight: 140,000kg/137.8 tons
Dimensions: Length – 10.27m/33ft 8in
  Height (over turret hatch) – 3.29m/10ft 10in
  Width – 4.48m/14ft 8in
Armament: Main – 17.2cm/6.77in gun
  Secondary – 7.5cm/2.95in gun and a 7.92mm/0.312in machine-gun
Armour: Maximum – 240mm/9.45in
Powerplant: Maybach HL234, V12 petrol, 521.9kW/700hp (for trials only)
Performance: Speed – 40kph/24.9mph
  Range – 120km/74.6 miles

FCM 36 Infantry Tank

The French FCM 36 was produced in 1936 as a light infantry support tank using welded armour. It was armed with a 37mm/1.46in low-velocity main gun and a 7.55mm/0.297in machine-gun in an octagonal turret, which had a non-rotating commander's position on the top. Powered by an 8.4-litre Berliet water-cooled diesel engine (the first French tank to be diesel powered), it had a top speed of 24kph/15mph and a radius of action of about 225km/140 miles. A distinctive feature of this vehicle was the skirting plates with mud chutes fitted over the upper half of the tracks.

When the manufacturers raised the unit price, the French Army curtailed their order to 100 vehicles, which were built between 1936–39 and saw action between May and June 1940. Combat proved it to be severely under-gunned and many were captured by the Germans who, appreciating this vehicle's range, modified them into a gun carriage, mounting the Krupp 10.5cm/4.1in leFH18 gun in an armoured superstructure on top of the original chassis.

ABOVE: The Char FCM 36 was a French infantry support tank built in 1936, and mounting a 37mm/1.46in gun and machine-gun in an octagonal-shaped turret. It was the first French tank to be powered by a diesel engine. BELOW: These FCM 36s were on parade in Paris on July 14, 1939, the last Bastille Day before war came. BOTTOM LEFT: The diesel engine for this tank was made in France under licence from Ricardo, who had made engines for some of the first British tanks during World War I.

FCM 36 Infantry Tank

Entered service: 1936
Crew: 2
Weight: 12,350kg/12.15 tons
Dimensions: Length – 4.22m/13ft 10m
    Height (over turret hatch) – 2.15m/7ft 0.61in
    Width – 1.95m/6ft 4.75in
Armament: Main – 37mm/1.46in gun
    Secondary – 7.55mm/0.297in machine-gun
Armour: Maximum – 40mm/1.57in
Powerplant: Berliet 8.4-litre, 4-cylinder diesel,
    67.9kW/91hp
Performance: Speed – 24kph/15mph
    Range – 225km/140 miles

Ford 3 Ton Tank

Entered service: 1918
Crew: 2
Weight: 3,150kg/3.1 tons
Dimensions: Length – 4.17m/13ft 8in
　Height (over turret hatch) – 1.60m/5ft 3in
　Width – 1.68m/5ft 6in
Armament: Main – 7.62mm/0.3in machine-gun
Armour: Maximum – 13mm/0.51in
Powerplant: 2 x Ford Model T 4-cylinder petrol, 33.58kW/45hp
Performance: Speed – 13kph/8mph
　Range – Unknown

Ford 3 Ton Tank

The US Army tank battalions that saw action in France during World War I were equipped with either British heavy tanks or French light tanks. In 1918, Ford built a two-man tank using the same characteristics and basic design of the highly successful French Renault FT-17. It was the cheapest and smallest tank built in the USA and undoubtedly the most successful. It was powered by two electrically started Model T Ford engines, producing 33.58kW/45hp between them, with the driver seated at the front and the steering being controlled through variation of the gear ratios of each engine. The gunner also was positioned at the front, armed with a 7.62mm/0.3in machine-gun in a limited-traverse mount. A prototype was sent to France and arrived in time to be tested and approved before the Armistice. Although over 15,000 were originally ordered, only 15 vehicles were actually ever built.

Ford 6 Ton Tank (M1917)

Entered service: 1917
Crew: 2
Weight: 6,574kg/6.47 tons
Dimensions: Length – 5.0m/16ft 5in
　Height (over turret hatch) – 2.3m/7ft 7in
　Width – 1.9m/6ft 3in
Armament: Main – 1 x 37mm/1.46in cannon or 1 x Colt 7.62mm/0.3in machine-gun
Armour: Maximum – 17mm/0.67in
Powerplant: Buda HU modified 4-cylinder petrol, 31.34kW/42hp
Performance: Speed – 9kph/5.6mph
　Range – 48km/29.8 miles

Ford 6 Ton Tank (M1917)

Copied directly from the French Renault FT-17 tank, this vehicle's official name was the M1917, but was known initially as the 6 Ton Special Tractor for security reasons. Although nearly 1,000 of these tanks were built, only 64 had been finished before the end of the war, and of these only 10 reached France. There were numerous improvements over the French design, including replacing the steel-rimmed wooden idler wheels on the Renault with all-steel ones, fitting a self-starter to the 4-cylinder engine and constructing a bulkhead between the crew and the engine compartment.

They continued in service for many years, and like the Liberty tank (the British Mark VIII), they were given to Canada for training purposes in 1939.

Hotchkiss H-35 Light Tank

LEFT: **The Hotchkiss H-35 was a** *char leger* **(cavalry tank) and thus considered by some French infantry as unsuitable. Nevertheless, it did come into service, many seeing action in France in 1940, with large numbers being captured and used extensively by the Germans.**

Hotchkiss H-35 Light Tank	
Entered service: 1936	
Crew: 2	
Weight: 10,600kg/10.43 tons	
Dimensions: Length – 4.22m/13ft 10in	
Height (over turret hatch) – 2.62m/8ft 7in	
Width – 1.96m/6ft 5in	
Armament: Main – 37mm/1.46in gun	
Secondary – 7.5mm/0.295in machine-gun	
Armour: Maximum – 40mm/1.58m	
Powerplant: Hotchkiss 1935, 6-cylinder, 55.91kW/75hp	
Performance: Speed – 27.4kph/17mph	
Range – 150km/93.2 miles	

Following demands from the French Cavalry for a light tank, the Hotchkiss H-35 was designed in 1933 and entered service in 1936, at which time its role was expanded to that of an infantry support tank. In the end some 400 were manufactured, with three quarters allotted to the Cavalry and the remaining quarter to the Infantry.

However, with its short-barrelled 37mm/1.46in main gun and single machine-gun as armament and its poor speed, its combat performance was disappointing against German armour. Under-gunned and underpowered, its sole advantage was its thick cast armour in the hull and turret. Commandeered by the Germans, the remaining H-35s had their turrets removed and were used as "schleppers" – to haul artillery and munitions. The turrets were incorporated into static defence lines.

Hotchkiss H-39 Light Tank

LEFT: **A line of brand new H-39s being prepared for issue. This little light tank was a development of the H-35 but had a new engine and a long-barrelled 37mm/1.46in gun. Like the H-35, it was also captured and used by the Germans, both in Russia and the Mediterranean theatre. Some H-39s were still in use by the Israelis in 1956.**

Hotchkiss H-39 Light Tank	
Entered service: 1939	
Crew: 2	
Weight: 12,100kg/11.9 tons	
Dimensions: Length – 4.23m/13ft 10in	
Height (over turret hatch) – 2.16m/7ft 1in	
Width – 1.96m/6ft 5in	
Armament: Main – 37mm/1.46in gun	
Secondary – 7.5mm/0.295in machine-gun	
Armour: Maximum – 40mm/1.57in	
Powerplant: Hotchkiss 1938, 6-cylinder petrol, 89.5kW/120hp	
Performance: Speed – 36.5kph/22.7mph	
Range – 150km/93.2 miles	

Between the H-35 and H-39 there was an interim model, the H-38. It sported a new, more powerful 89.5kW/120hp petrol engine which improved its mobility but still had the same ineffectual 37mm/1.46in main gun. It was only in the final model of the series, the H-39, that the main armament, though remaining the same calibre, was upgraded to a long-barrelled variant.

This vehicle did not fare long or well against the Germans in 1940 who, as with its predecessors, removed the turret to use it as a tractor to haul artillery and munitions. Radio sets were fitted with a 2m/6ft 6in-long rod aerial mounted on a tripod on the front right-hand mudguard. It was used by the Germans both in the Russian and Mediterranean theatres.

JS-1 Heavy Tank

JS-1 Heavy Tank	
Entered service: 1943	
Crew: 4	
Weight: 46.000kg/45.3 tons	
Dimensions: Length – 8.32m/27ft 3in	
Height (over turret hatch) – 2.9m/9ft 6in	
Width – 3.25m/10ft 8in	
Armament: Main – 100mm/3.94in gun	
Secondary – 2 x 7.62mm/0.3in machine-guns	
Armour: Maximum – 132mm/5.2in	
Powerplant: V2-IS 12-cylinder diesel, 382.8kW/510hp	
Performance: Speed – 40kph/24.9mph	
Range – 250km/155 miles	

Hard on the heels of the KV-1, Russia began to develop a new tank in 1941, to cope with the new German tanks that had appeared in response to both it and the T-34 in the race for battlefield supremacy. At that time, the requirement was for a four-man tank with an 85mm/3.35in gun and sufficient armour to keep out the German 50mm/ 1.97in anti-tank gun round, but with no significant increase in weight over the KV-1 series. By the time the JS-1 appeared in 1943, the main armament had been changed from 85mm/3.34in to 100mm/3.94in. Basically an enlarged superstructure over a KV chassis enabled the fitting of a larger turret ring and turret to accommodate the larger main gun. This tank had a very good ballistic shape, a low silhouette and was very reliable. In late 1944 a small number had their 100mm/3.94in gun replaced with a 122mm/4.8in gun in a larger turret.

JS-2 Heavy Tank

JS-2 Heavy Tank	
Entered service: 1944	
Crew: 4	
Weight: 46,000kg/45.3 tons	
Dimensions: Length – 9.9m/32ft 6in	
Height (over turret hatch) – 2.73m/8ft 11in	
Width – 3.09m/10ft 2in	
Armament: Main – 122mm/4.8in D-25 gun	
Secondary – 3 x 7.62mm/0.3in machine-guns	
Armour: Maximum – 120mm/4.72in	
Powerplant: V2-IS 12-cylinder diesel, 382.8kW/513hp	
Performance: Speed – 37kph/23mph	
Range – 240km/149 miles	

The next model in the JS series appeared in 1944, an improved model of the JS-1, but with little external difference other than the 122mm/4.8in main gun which now became standard. This made the JS-2 the most powerfully armed tank in the world at that time. It had a smaller cupola and some differences in the armour silhouette around the front hull. The JS-2 was known as the Victory Tank, and led on to the JS-3. It was undoubtedly the most advanced heavy tank of its time and had a major influence on Western tank design. The JS-2 was accepted for production at the end of December 1943, and by the beginning of 1944 some 100 were in operational service.

KV-1 Heavy Tank

The KV-1 Heavy Tank with which Russia entered World War II was, along with the T-34, the closest any Allied forces came to armour parity with the Germans at that time. It was basically a redesign of the T-100, with one its turrets eliminated. Named after the Russian defence commissar Marshal Klimenti Voroshilov, it first saw active service in the Russo-Finnish war. It was replaced a little later, in 1940, by the KV-1A, which mounted a better gun with a higher muzzle velocity and firing a larger round – the 76.2mm/3in L/41.5 Model 40. This firepower combined with thick armour stunned the Germans when they first encountered it. A special diagnostic team from Germany was rushed to the front to analyse both it and the T-34. However, it was let down by its unreliable transmission, and this, coupled with its weight, made it difficult to drive, slow and cumbersome. Production ceased in 1943.

LEFT: **The KV-1 Heavy Tank gave the Germans a shock when they first encountered it during the opening weeks of their assault on the USSR because they had summarily discounted the Red Army's heavy tanks as being both old-fashioned and obsolete. This one, having been captured in the Russo-Finnish war, still has a Finnish swastika on its turret.**

KV-1 Heavy Tank

Entered service: 1939
Crew: 5
Weight: 43,000kg/42.3 tons
Dimensions: Length – 6.68m/21ft 11in
  Height (over turret hatch) – 2.71m/8ft 11in
  Width – 3.32m/10ft 11in
Armament: Main – 76.2mm/3in L/41 ZiS-5 gun
  Secondary – up to 4 x 7.62mm/0.3in
  machine-guns
Armour: Maximum – 75mm/2.95in
Powerplant: V2K V12 diesel, 410kW/550bhp
Performance: Speed – 35kph/21.7mph
  Range – 150km/93 miles

KV-2 Heavy Tank

KV-2 Heavy Tank

Entered service: 1940
Crew: 6
Weight: 53,963kg/53.1 tons
Dimensions: Length – 6.79m/22ft 3in
  Height (over turret hatch) – 3.65m/12ft
  Width – 3.32m/10ft 11in
Armament: Main – 152mm/5.98in L/20 howitzer
  Secondary – 2 x 7.62mm/0.3in machine-guns
Armour: Maximum – 110mm/4.33in
Powerplant: V2K V12 diesel, 410kW/550bhp
Performance: Speed – 26kph/16mph
  Range – 150km/93 miles

LEFT: **The close-support version of the KV-1 was known as the KV-2, and mounted a massive 152mm/5.98in howitzer in a large slab-sided turret. This captured KV-2 is being inspected by the Germans.**

The KV-2 was a specialized tank developed to break through fortifications similar to the Funnies being developed in the Western theatre by the British. A huge 152mm/5.98in howitzer was mounted in a gargantuan turret and could fire a special dustbin-sized anti-concrete shell to destroy bastions and pillboxes. There was an extra crew member in the turret to help operate this weapon system, pushing the crew total up to six.

The chassis and engine were the same as that of the KV-1, which made it even slower and more vulnerable than its predecessor, and the Germans quickly learned to aim for its tracks to first immobilize and then destroy it.

The No. 1 Lincoln Machine "Little Willie"

Designed by William Tritton (later Sir), chief executive of William Foster and Co. Ltd of Lincoln, and Lt W. G. Wilson, then an RNAS (Royal Naval Air Service) armoured car officer, the "Tritton Machine", as it was sometimes called, was designed and constructed between August 2 and September 8, 1915. It weighed 18,290kg/18 tons, and above its rectangular hull was to have been a centrally mounted turret with a 2pdr gun; however, this was never fitted and a dummy turret of the correct weight was used when the machine was tested.

The machine had Bullock tracks, brought from America, where they had been developed commercially from an original British design. Tail wheels helped the cross-country performance and aided steering.

The first version prototype of the No. 1 Lincoln Machine suffered from track problems, through a lack of grip and an inclination for the tracks to come off when crossing trenches. Speed was between 3.2–4.8kph/2–3mph. It could just about cross a 1.2m/4ft wide trench and mount a 0.61m/2ft vertical step.

ABOVE: **The very first tank to be built in the world – "Little Willie", the No. 1 Lincoln Machine – which was designed and completed in 1915.** RIGHT: **This was the No. 1 Lincoln Machine as designed by Tritton and Wilson, utilizing Bullock tracks and a dummy turret. It was modified to become "Little Willie" by using different tracks. Note also the rear steering wheels.**

In order to meet new War Office revised requirements to cross a 1.52m/5ft trench and climb a 1.37m/4.5ft step, the No. 1 Lincoln Machine had to be rebuilt, using the original hull and engine (a 6-cylinder Daimler petrol engine, developing 78.29kW/105bhp), but with completely redesigned tracks. The new tracks had their frames increased in length and comprised cast steel plates riveted to links which had guides engaging with rails on the side of the track frames. This pattern of track construction was used for all British tanks up to 1918 to improve cross-country performance. The simulated turret was also removed, and "Little Willie" was completed early in December 1915. (Presumably the name had some ribald connection with Kaiser Wilhelm II.)

The No. 1 Lincoln Machine "Little Willie"

Entered service: 1915 (prototype only)
Crew: 4–6
Weight: 18,290kg/18 tons
Dimensions: Length – 5.53m/18ft 2in
  Height (over turret hatch) – 3.1m/10ft 2in
  Width – 2.85m/9ft 4in
Armament: Main – 2pdr (40mm/1.57in) gun
  Secondary – 1 x 7.7mm/0.303in Maxim
  machine-gun and up to 3 x 7.7mm/0.303in
  Lewis machine-guns
Armour: Maximum – 6mm/0.24in
Powerplant: Daimler 6-cylinder petrol, generating
  78.29kW/105bhp
Performance: Speed – 3.2kph/2mph
  Range – Unknown

LK I Light Tank

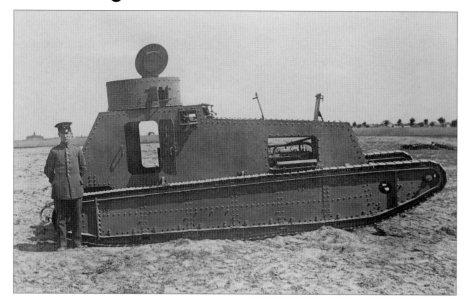

LEFT: **The LK I was a relatively simple tank, with a Daimler car chassis and axles for its suspension. It was only ever produced in prototype form in mid-1918.**

LK I Light Tank

Entered service: 1918 (prototype only)
Crew: 3
Weight: 7,000kg/6.89 tons
Dimensions: Length – 5.49m/18ft
   Height (over turret hatch) – 2.48m/8ft 2in
   Width – 2m/6ft 7in
Armament: Main – 1 x 7.92mm/0.312in machine-gun
   Secondary – None
Armour: Maximum – 8mm/0.31in
Powerplant: 4-cylinder petrol, 44.7kW/60bhp
Performance: Speed – 13kph/8mph
   Range – 64km/40 miles

The German light tank LK I (*Leichte Kampfwagen I*) was designed in mid-1918 by Joseph Vollmer, who had also worked on the A7V. He advocated the use of simple, light tanks that were easy and cheap to produce in preference to large, heavy and expensive ones. The LK I only reached prototype stage before the Armistice. Using a Daimler car chassis as well as other automotive parts (such as axles for the sprocket and idler wheels), it followed the normal layout of an automobile, weighed nearly 7 tons, had a three-man crew and was armed with one 7.92mm/0.312in machine-gun.

LK II Light Tank

LEFT: **The *Leichte Kampfwagen II* was produced from the LK I. It had thicker armour and a 57mm/ 2.24in gun, but was still a relatively simple tank. Two prototypes were built, but the subsequent order for 580 never materialized, because World War I ended. The design was passed to Sweden and used as the basis of their Strv M/21 Light Tank.**

LK II Light Tank

Entered service: 1918
Crew: 3
Weight: 8,890kg/8.75 tons
Dimensions: Length – 5.1m/16ft 9in
   Height (over turret hatch) – 2.49m/8ft 2in
   Width – 1.98m/6ft 6in
Armament: Main – 1 x 57mm/2.24in gun or
   2 x 7.92mm/0.312in machine-guns
Armour: Maximum – 14mm/0.55in
Powerplant: Daimler-Benz, 4-cylinder petrol,
   44.7kW/60hp
Performance: Speed – 12kph/7.5mph
   Range – 64.4km/40 miles

An LK II was then designed from the LK I, mounting a larger 57mm/ 2.24in main gun and weighing almost 2,000kg/2 tons more due to its thicker armour, but otherwise being similar to its predecessor. It also did not get further than prototype stage. A variant carrying two 7.92mm/0.312in machine-guns in a traversing turret was also proposed but never built, for although two gun-armed LK II prototypes were manufactured, the planned production run of 580 was terminated by the Armistice of November 1918. After 1918, the LK II drawings were passed to Sweden and used to manufacture their Strv M/21 of 1921.

Medium B Whippet

The shape of the Medium B was more like that of the heavy tank than its predecessor, the Medium A Whippet, but with a large fixed turret mounted on top at the front of the hull. The Medium B weighed 18,289kg/18 tons and was longer and wider than the Medium A, but not so tall. The engine, a 6-cylinder 74.57kW/100hp Ricardo, was mounted in a separate compartment, with a bulkhead to divide it from the crew of four – the first tank ever to have this feature.

BELOW LEFT: **Built in 1918, the shape of the Medium B Whippet reverted back to the earlier rhomboidal design. The Armistice led to the cancellation of the order; however, 17 of the 45 built were sent to Russia in 1919, to support the White Russians against the Bolsheviks.**

Medium B Whippet

Entered service: 1918
Crew: 4
Weight: 18,289kg/18 tons
Dimensions: Length – 6.93m/22ft 9in
   Height (over turret hatch) – 2.59m/8ft 6in
   Width – 2.69m/8ft 10in
Armament: Main – 4 x 7.7mm/0.303in Hotchkiss machine-guns
Armour: Maximum – 14mm/0.55in
Powerplant: Ricardo 6-cylinder petrol, 74.57kW/100hp
Performance: Speed – 12.7kph/7.9mph
   Range – Approximately 64km/40 miles

Medium C Hornet

Although it was designed in late 1917, none of the 45 Medium Cs built actually left the factory until after the Armistice. They remained in service until 1925, and proved to be remarkably effective tanks, with a better performance than any of the previous Mediums.

The Medium C had a fixed turret armed with four Hotchkiss 7.7mm/0.303in machine-guns, and a rotating commander's cupola. At 20,320kg/20 tons, its rear-mounted 111.8kW/150hp Ricardo engine gave it a power-to-weight ratio of 7.5, while its fuel tanks held 682 litres/150 gallons – over double that of the Medium A. Top speed was still only 12.9kph/8mph and its radius of action was 121km/75 miles.

The very last tank to be designed in World War I was the Medium Mark D, which never got further than the design stage. However, various modified models were produced after the war, the Johnson Light Infantry Tank being based on the Medium D design. It also had a fixed turret with three ball-mounted machine-guns sited ahead of the driver who sat at the rear above the gunners' stations, steering by means of a small conning tower. There was also a new wire rope suspension system to improve its speed.

LEFT: **Designed by Tritton in late 1917, the Hornet, as the Medium C was also called, resembled the Medium B (engine at rear), but incorporated all the wartime experience of the tank crews, so it was considerably improved.**

Medium C Hornet

Entered service: 1918
Crew: 4
Weight: 20,320kg/20 tons
Dimensions: Length – 7.92m/26ft
   Height (over turret hatch) – 3.00m/9ft 6in
   Width – 2.54m/8ft 4in
Armament: Main – 4 x 7.7mm/0.303in Hotchkiss machine-guns
Armour: Maximum – 14mm/0.55in
Powerplant: Ricardo 6-cylinder petrol, 111.8kW/150hp
Performance: Speed – 12.9kph/8mph
   Range – 121km/75 miles

Medium A Whippet

Designed by Sir William Tritton in November 1916, the Medium A, also known as the Whippet or the Tritton Chaser, was the only British medium tank to see action during World War I. Construction began in December 1916 at William Foster's factory in Lincoln, and trials were held on February 11, 1917, after which an order was placed for 200 tanks four months later.

The tank ran on two 33.6kW/45hp 4-cylinder Tyler lorry engines – one for each track, with dual ignition. It also had twin four-speed gearboxes and clutches, making it very difficult to handle and seriously increasing servicing time. Gentle steering, such as on roads, was by means of a column which controlled the throttle on each engine – and thus each track, accelerating one and retarding the other automatically. For serious turning, especially on cross-country, the gearboxes had to be used.

Seventy gallons of fuel was carried, contained in a drum-shaped tank in the front of the machine (under armour-plating) and was fed to the engines by an autovac system. The tracks were half-round, like those on "Little Willie". There was no unditching beam, but instead there were two towing shackles, and oak spuds were provided. For observation, there were three rotary peephole covers and three periscope openings.

ABOVE: **The Tank Museum's Whippet. This was the tank, nicknamed Caesar, on which Lt Sewell won his Victoria Cross on April 29, 1918.** LEFT: **One of Sewell's No. 9 Section, 3rd (Light) Tank Battalion, which he commanded in 1918.**

The first Whippets to see action did so on March 26, 1918, at Hebuterne, during the Second Battle of the Somme. They continued to perform sterling work right up to the Armistice; indeed, one of the Tank Corps Victoria Crosses was awarded to Lieutenant Cecil Sewell while he was commanding his Whippet, Caesar II, A 253, which is now on show at the Tank Museum, Bovington, England.

The official account of his action says, "This officer displayed the greatest gallantry and initiative in getting out of his own tank and crossing open ground under heavy shell and machine-gun fire to rescue the crew of another Whippet of his section which had side-slipped into a large shell hole, overturned and taken fire." After releasing the crew, Sewell then dashed back across open ground to assist one of his own crew, and a few minutes later he was hit again, this time fatally, while dressing his driver's wounds. He showed "utter disregard for his own personal safety".

ABOVE LEFT: **Good view of the open rear door of a 3rd Battalion Whippet. Two hundred of these 14,225kg/14-ton tanks were built.** ABOVE: **A quartet of Medium A Whippets take part in the Armistice Day parade in Central London as part of a large tank column.** BELOW: **The lighter, faster Whippet was ideal for exploiting the successes of the heavy tanks – a sort of armoured cavalry.**

Medium A Whippet

Entered service: 1917

Crew: 3

Weight: 14,225kg/14 tons

Dimensions: Length – 6.10m/20ft
  Height (over turret hatch) – 2.74m/9ft
  Width – 2.62m/8ft 7in

Armament: 4 x 7.7mm/0.303 Hotchkiss
  machine-guns

Armour: Maximum – 14mm/0.55in

Powerplant: 2 x Taylor JB4 petrol, each developing
  33.6kW/45hp

Performance: Speed – 12.9kph/8mph
  Range – 64.4km/40 miles

Mark I Heavy Tank "Mother"

Even while "Little Willie" was being built, Tritton and Wilson were working on a new design, which had a much longer track length in order to improve its cross-country performance and – to be sure of meeting the new War Office requirements – to cross a 1.52m/5ft trench and climb a 1.22m/4ft step. It had been worked out that this could be achieved by a wheel 1.83m/6ft in diameter, so the length of the track on the ground and its shape had to be the same as the lower curve of a wheel of that size. This meant raising the height of the front horns, and gave rise to the now familiar rhomboidal shape common to all of the British World War I heavy tanks. In order to keep the centre of gravity low, it was decided to mount the tank's main armament – two naval 6pdr guns – in side sponsons. During her life, "Mother" had various names such as "Big Willie" and "HMLS Centipede", but as the very first battle tank she was rightly called "Mother" – despite her Male armament (Female tanks had two extra machine-guns instead of 6pdrs so they were about a ton lighter).

ABOVE: **"Clan Leslie" a British Heavy Tank Mark I (Male). Note the long-barrelled 6pdr naval gun in its side sponson. A total of 150 of these tanks were built, the basic design being exactly the same as for "Mother".**
LEFT: **Mark I Male tank D7 (No. 742) commanded by Lt Enoch pauses after the Flers Battle.**

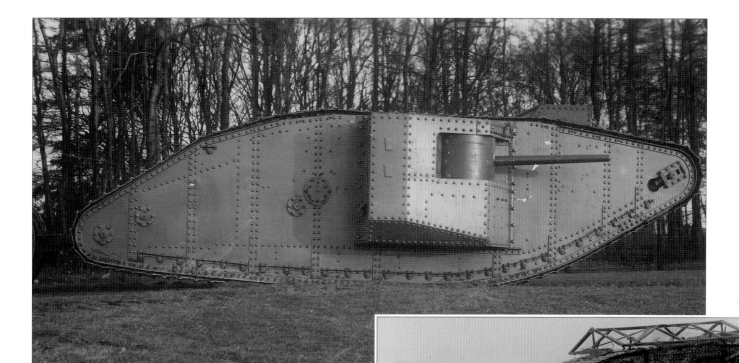

The building of the first batch of 100 Mark I tanks began in February 1916, following the same basic design as "Mother". They were called "tanks" for security reasons, to disguise their true purpose. Half of the first batch was Male tanks with 6pdr guns, the rest Female with two machine-guns in each sponson.

It was not until after the first tank versus tank engagement in April 1918 that the danger of having a tank with no effective weapon capable of penetrating an enemy tank was realized, and thereafter hermaphrodite tanks with one 6pdr sponson and one dual machine-gun sponson were introduced. The Mark I was recognizable by its tail wheels to assist with steering, the unshortened barrel on its ex-Naval 6pdr guns and the anti-grenade "roof" made of chicken wire.

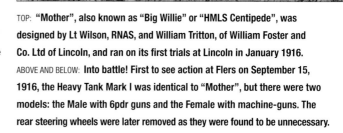

TOP: "Mother", also known as "Big Willie" or "HMLS Centipede", was designed by Lt Wilson, RNAS, and William Tritton, of William Foster and Co. Ltd of Lincoln, and ran on its first trials at Lincoln in January 1916.

ABOVE AND BELOW: Into battle! First to see action at Flers on September 15, 1916, the Heavy Tank Mark I was identical to "Mother", but there were two models: the Male with 6pdr guns and the Female with machine-guns. The rear steering wheels were later removed as they were found to be unnecessary.

Mark I Heavy Tank "Mother" (Male)

Entered service: 1916
Crew: 8
Weight: 28,450kg/28 tons
Dimensions: Length – 9.9m/32ft 6in
    Height (over turret hatch) – 2.41m/7ft 11in
    Width – 4.19m/13ft 9in
Armament: Main – 2 x 6pdr (57mm/2.24in) guns
    Secondary – 7.7mm/0.303in Hotchkiss
    machine-gun
Armour: Maximum – 12mm/0.47in
Powerplant: Daimler 6-cylinder petrol,
    111.8kW/150bhp
Performance: Speed – 5.95kph/3.7mph
    Range – 35.4km/22 miles

Mark I Medium Tank

Following on from the Medium D, this Vickers-built 12,192kg/12-ton tank was originally called Light Tank Mark I and was the first British tank designed after World War I, with production models coming into service in 1924. It was later reclassified as Mark I Medium Tank and

LEFT: **Mediums on training. The Mark I remained in operational service until 1938 and was thereafter only used for training.**

was the first British tank to have all-round traverse capability and geared elevation for the main gun, a 3pdr (47mm/1.85in), a 94mm/3.7in howitzer being fitted in the close-support tanks. Two Vickers machine-guns were ball-mounted in the hull sides, while there were four Hotchkiss machine-guns carried in the turret for dismounted use. The crew was five (commander, driver, radio-operator and two gunners). Spring suspension enabled it to achieve a higher speed than previous designs, the 67.1kW/90hp air-cooled Armstrong Siddeley V8 engine giving it a top speed of 24kph/15mph. Production of the Mark I and II amounted to some 160 in total.

ABOVE: **The Mark I Medium Tank was the first British tank to be designed after World War I, and to reach production. It had a fully traversing turret and its main armament could be elevated. This rear view has the turret traversed rear and the rear door open.**

Mark I Medium Tank	

Entered service: 1924

Crew: 5

Weight: 12,192kg/12 tons

Dimensions: Length – 5.33m/17ft 6in
Height (over turret hatch) – 2.82m/9ft 3in
Width – 2.79m/9ft 2in

Armament: Main – 3pdr (47mm/1.85in) gun
Secondary – 2 x 7.7mm/0.303in Vickers machine-guns and 4 x Hotchkiss 7.7mm/0.303in machine-guns

Armour: Maximum – 8mm/0.315in

Powerplant: Armstrong-Siddeley V8 petrol, developing 67.1kW/90hp

Performance: Speed – 24kph/15mph
Range – 241km/150 miles

Mark II and Mark III Heavy Tanks

In all, some 150 Mark I Heavy Tanks were produced and delivered to the Army. As a result of their impact upon the battlefield, the Commander-in-Chief Field-Marshal Sir Douglas Haig ordered a further 1,000 tanks to be built. First of these were 50 Mark IIs – 25 Male and 25 Female. They were almost identical to the Mark I apart from minor alterations resulting from the limited battle experience of the Mark Is on the Somme.

The tail wheels were discarded, there was a revised hatch on top, and a wider track shoe at every sixth track link in order to improve traction. Armour on these early tanks had to be cut and drilled as soft steel and then hardened to inhibit hostile fire. The front plates were 10mm/0.394in thick, the sides 8mm/ 0.315in. The tank was built by riveting sheets of armour plate to butt straps and angle iron. Inevitably, there were gaps,

which allowed molten metal to penetrate inside when a joint was hit by small arms fire. This "splash", as it was called, meant that the crew had to wear small

steel masks with a chain-mail visor hanging down over the face, to reduce injury. However, they were uncomfortable to wear and made it much more difficult to observe, so the crews would hang blankets inside to absorb the splash.

The Mark III Heavy Tank was virtually identical to the Mark II except that it had slightly thicker armour. Fifty Mark IIIs (half of them Male and half Female) were built. The later Males were armed with the short-barrelled 6pdr gun because naval guns proved too long for land use, banging into trees or becoming buried in the mud. Guns could fire either High-Explosive or Armour-Piercing shot.

BELOW: **Apart from having slightly thicker armour, the Mark III was identical to the Mark II. Only 50 were built (half Male and half Female).**

Mark III Heavy Tank (Male)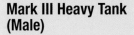

Entered service: 1917
Crew: 8
Weight: 28,450kg/28 tons
Dimensions: Length – 9.9m/32ft 6in
    Height (over turret hatch) – 2.41m/7ft 11in
    Width – 4.19m/13ft 9in
Armament: Male – 2 x 6pdr (57mm/2.24in) guns
    Female – 2 x Hotchkiss 7.7mm/0.303in machine-guns
Armour: Maximum – 12mm/0.47in
Powerplant: Daimler 6-cylinder petrol, developing 111.8kW/150bhp
Performance: Speed – 5.95kph/3.7mph
    Range – 35.4km/22 miles

Mark II Medium Tank

The Mark II Medium Tank shared many features with the Mark I Medium, using the same basic chassis, engine and armament. They also both had the sprung "box bogie" suspension which gave the Mark II a speed of 40–48kph/ 25–30mph, far in advance of its theoretical design speed of around 29kph/18mph. However, the extra weight of the Mark II reduced the top speed to around 24kph/15mph. Armament comprised the 3pdr gun, plus two Vickers machine-guns in the hull sides and three Hotchkiss machine-guns projecting out around the turret.

There were other differences between the Marks. Externally, the Mark IIs appeared much bulkier, the armour was thicker, the superstructure was a little higher, and the driver's hood stood proud of the hull top. Also, the driver's glacis was steeper, the headlights larger and the Mark IIs had suspension skirts. The major mechanical difference was in the steering, with the Mark II having Rackham Steering, with an additional epicyclic gearbox between the main gearbox and the differential cum cross-shaft.

ABOVE: **A line of Mediums firing on the Gunnery School Ranges at Lulworth, Dorset. This is still the "home" of tank gunnery, now as part of the British Army Armour Centre.** BELOW: **The Tank Museum's Vickers Mark II* Medium Tank. Entering service in 1926, the Royal Tank Corps was pleased to receive these modern tanks, although they probably did not realize that they would stay in active service until after the beginning of World War II!**

In 1932, modifications were made to the Medium Mark II, resulting in the Marks II* and II**. In the former, the three Hotchkiss machine-guns in the turret were replaced by a single coaxial Vickers, while the commander's cupola was set further back in the turret roof. A lead counterweight was added at the back of the turret. In the latter, the wireless was placed in an armoured container and attached at the back of the turret.

A total of 160 Mark II Mediums were built and were used for training after war was declared, but never saw action. Latterly, some of those in Egypt were buried up to their turrets at Mersa Matruh as static pillboxes. The Tank Museum's Mark II* was restored to full running order by Vickers Defence Systems in the 1980s.

Mark II Medium Tank	
Entered service: 1925	
Crew: 5	
Weight: 14,224kg/14 tons	
Dimensions: Length – 5.33m/17ft 6in	
Height (over turret hatch) – 2.69m/8ft 10in	
Width – 2.79m/9ft 2in	
Armament: Main – 3pdr (47mm/1.85in) gun	
Secondary – 3 x 7.7mm/0.303 Vickers machine-guns (1 x coaxial replacing 3 x Hotchkiss)	
Armour: Maximum – 12mm/0.47in	
Powerplant: Armstrong-Siddley 8-cylinder petrol, developing 67.1kW/90hp	
Performance: Speed – 24kph/15mph	
Range – 193km/120 miles	

Mark II and Mark III Light Tanks

LEFT: Following on from the Mark I Light Tank came the Mark II, which appeared in 1931 and had the Horstmann coil spring suspension, which improved its cross-country performance.

British light and medium tank development began with the Whippet, which was created to provide a fast cavalry or pursuit tank to exploit any opportunity or breakthrough by the heavy tanks. Later, after the war, light tanks or tankettes were built to help mechanize the infantry. However, with the advent of these small, fast and low-silhouette vehicles, a new concept for

their use was found, namely to provide reconnaissance for the heavier tanks. Turreted versions of the Carden-Loyd were developed and known as Patrol Tanks Marks I and II.

During the mid-1930s and after having taken over Carden-Loyd, Vickers-Armstrong spent much time and effort in the development of light tanks. Initially a series of two-man machines (Marks I–IV)

LEFT: Following on from the Mark I Light Tank came the Mark II, which appeared in 1931 and had the Horstmann coil spring suspension, which improved its cross-country performance.

mounting a single Vickers machine-gun, they were later enlarged into three-man light tanks armed with two machine-guns in a two-man turret. These light AFVs were perfect for patrolling the border provinces of the far-flung British Empire.

The Mark II was based on the Mark I, with the same hull, but having a larger rectangular turret, the No. 1 Mark I, and with a new, more powerful Rolls-Royce 6-cylinder engine replacing the Meadows of its predecessor. It was fitted with Horstmann spring coil suspension.

The next two Marks – the IIA and IIB – were fitted with the No. 1 Mark II turret, modified with air louvers on the sides for hot climates. A difference between the two was that the Mark IIA had an extra fuel tank fitted and the Mark IIB a single large-capacity tank of the same capacity as the Mark IIA. Entering service in 1933, the Mark III was the same as its predecessors other than having an extended rear superstructure to accommodate a modified Horstmann suspension system which had evolved from a two-pair to four-pair type.

LEFT: Entering service in 1933, the Mark III Light Tank was similar in layout to the Mark II, but had its superstructure extended rearwards and was fitted with a modified Horstmann suspension.

Mark II Light Tank

Entered service: 1931
Crew: 2
Weight: 4572kg/4.5 tons
Dimensions: Length – 3.58m/11ft 9in
    Height (over turret hatch) – 2.01m/6ft 7in
    Width – 1.91m/6ft 3in
Armament: Main – 7.7mm/0.303in Vickers machine-gun
Armour: Maximum – 10mm/0.39in
Powerplant: Rolls-Royce 6-cylinder, 49.2kW/66bhp
Performance: Speed – 48.3kph/30mph
    Range – 209.2km/130 miles

Mark III Valentine Infantry Tank

The prototype of the Valentine was produced by Vickers on February 14, 1940, hence its name. Over 8,000 Valentines were built in 11 different Marks, as well as various specialized variants, and it remained in production until 1944, being supplied to Russia and built under licence in Canada. This accounts for approximately a quarter of all British wartime tank production.

Over the course of its service life the Valentine's construction changed from being riveted to welded, and its power source from petrol to diesel – the AEC petrol and diesel engines being finally replaced with the more reliable GMC two-stroke diesel. It also had a variety of main armaments, beginning with the 2pdr, giving way to the 6pdr and then to the 75mm/2.95in on the final model. The Valentine saw most of its active service in the North African theatre, where extra fuel tanks attached to the rear increased its range, although it was also used by Commonwealth troops in the Pacific and Asian theatres.

Variants included a bridgelayer, flail and snake explosive-charge mine-sweepers, self-propelled guns, a flame-thrower and also an amphibious version.

ABOVE: **A modern photograph of the Bovington Tank Museum's Infantry Tank Mark III Valentine in desert colours. Developed by Vickers, it proved to be both strong and reliable.** BELOW LEFT: **In April 2004 Ex Smash was held at Studland Bay in Dorset, during which Mr John Pearson's wonderfully restored Valentine DD (Duplex Drive) went into the water from a landing craft to commemorate the loss of six crewmen of 4/7 DG back in 1944. The DD was also on show at the Tank Museum's "Tankfest" on May 23, 2004.**

Mark III Valentine Infantry Tank

Entered service: 1940
Crew: 3
Weight: 17,272kg/17 tons
Dimensions: Length – 5.89m/19ft 4in
   Height (over turret hatch) – 2.29m/7ft 6in
   Width – 2.64m/8ft 8in
Armament: Main – 2pdr (40mm/1.58in) or 6pdr (57mm/2.24in) or 75mm/2.95in gun
   Secondary – 7.92mm/0.312in Besa machine-gun
Armour: Maximum – 65mm/2.56in
Powerplant: AEC 6-cylinder diesel, 97.73kW/131bhp; or AEC 6-cylinder petrol, 100kW/135bhp; or GMC diesel, 100kW/135bhp
Performance: Speed – 24kph/14.9mph
   Range – 145km/90 miles

Mark IV Light Tank

Mark IV Light Tank

Entered service: 1934
Crew: 2
Weight: 4,674kg/4.6 tons
Dimensions: Length – 3.40m/11ft 2in
  Height (over turret hatch) – 2.13m/7ft
  Width – 2.06m/6ft 9in
Armament: 1 x 7.7mm/0.303in and
  1 x 12.7mm/0.5in machine-guns
Armour: Maximum – 12mm/0.47in
Powerplant: Meadows 6-cylinder petrol,
  65.6kW/88bhp
Performance: Speed – 56kph/35mph
  Range – 201km/125 miles

LEFT: **Built in the 1930s and based on the "Indian Pattern" light tanks, this Mark IV Light Tank now resides at the Tank Museum. The principal change to the Mark III was its suspension.**

The Mark IV Light Tank was based on the Vickers experimental "Indian Pattern" vehicles of 1933, being produced the following year. It was the first light tank that used the hull as a chassis, with its automotive parts then bolted on to it. The hull was lengthened, its armour thickened and it consequently had a higher superstructure with the turret set further back than other light tanks. The Horstmann suspension was modified to dispense with the idler wheel by re-spacing the bogies, which gave the vehicle a distinctive track path. The turret itself was similar to that of the Mark III Light Tank, but certain modifications were made, with a cupola variant for those vehicles bound for service in India.

Mark V Light Tank

Mark V Light Tank

Entered service: 1935
Crew: 3
Weight: 4,217kg/4.15 tons
Dimensions: Length – 3.68m/12ft 1in
  Height (over turret hatch) – 2.21m/7ft 3in
  Width – 2.06m/6ft 9in
Armament: 1 x 7.7mm/0.303in and
  1 x 12.7mm/0.5in Vickers machine-guns
Armour: Maximum – 12mm/0.5in
Powerplant: Meadows 6-cylinder petrol, developing
  65.6kW/88bhp
Performance: Speed – 51kph/32mph
  Range – 200km/125 miles

LEFT: **This Mark V Light Tank is being inspected by a visiting German delegation during the 1930s. It was the first of the light series to have a three-man crew (two men in the turret).**

Entering service in 1935, the Mark V Light Tank had a longer hull than its predecessor in order to accommodate a turret ball-race and then a larger two-man turret – the first on a light tank – raising the crew total to three. It was armed with Vickers 7.7mm/0.303in and 12.7mm/0.5in coaxial machine-guns and had a circular commander's cupola. With its heavier weight of 4,217kg/4.15 tons, its handling and characteristics were a big improvement on earlier Marks. However both the Mark IV and Mark V were obsolete at the start of World War II. A few remained, mostly used for training, though two chassis were used for experiments with anti-aircraft mounts in 1940.

Mark IV Heavy Tank

Designed in October 1916, the Mark IV was put into production between March and April 1917. More Mark IVs were built than any other model – a total of 1,220 – of which 205 were tank tenders with specially boosted 93.2kW/125bhp Daimler engines. The tenders were fitted with square box-like sponsons and used to carry tank supplies into battle.

The Mark IV had various improvements, including an armoured 273-litre/60-gallon petrol tank mounted outside the tank between the rear horns. This was much safer than the earlier internal tanks, which were located on either side of the driver. Sponsons were hinged so that they could be swung

TOP: **More Mark IV Heavy Tanks were built than any other model – a total of 1,220 in all. This is the Tank Museum's "HMS Excellent", which was restored to full running order in 1971 by 18 Command Workshop, REME.**
ABOVE: **This Mark IV Heavy Tank bears the letters "WC" for "Wire Cutter", but is being used as an observation platform, having lost part of its right-hand track.** BELOW LEFT: **Male Tank No. 2341 bore the "Chinese Eye" on its sides as it was paid for by Mr Eu Tong Sen of the Malay States. This custom is still retained today by the tanks and other AFVs of 1 RTR.**

inside during rail journeys, instead of having to be removed and carried separately. The size of the sponsons was also reduced so that the lower edges were not so close to the ground. In both versions, the Vickers and Hotchkiss machine-guns were replaced by Lewis guns, but these proved a great disappointment and later had to be replaced with modified Hotchkiss machine-guns. Thicker steel was used in the construction of the Mark IV – 12mm/0.47in in front and on the sides, decreasing to 8mm/0.315in elsewhere. This made it bullet-proof against the German anti-tank rifle. The first Mark IVs went into action on June 7, 1917, at the Battle of Messines Ridge.

However, it would be during the Battle of Cambrai on November 20, 1917, that they really showed their prowess, many of the 476 tanks taking part being heavy Mark IVs, whose silhouette now forms an indispensable part of

both the RTR cap and arm badges, while November 20 is celebrated every year as the RTR Regimental Day.

Many of the tank crews fighting at Cambrai had been trained with the invaluable help of the Royal Navy Gunnery Training Establishment at Whale Island, Portsmouth, so Mark IV Heavy Tank No. 2324 was presented to HMS *Excellent* in recognition on May 1, 1919. Twenty years later it was restored to full serviceability and allocated to the RN defence battalion, patrolling Portsmouth during air raids, until it damaged a private car and had to be confined to barracks!

ABOVE: **"Any more for the Skylark?" A crowd of footsore infantrymen cadge a lift on this Mark IV (Female), those at the rear resting their feet on the unditching beam.** BELOW: **Without its weapons fitted, this Mark IV Heavy Tank is recognizable as a Female by its smaller sponsons. The steel plate was proof against German armour-piercing "K" rounds.**

In 1971 it was decided to hand back the historic old tank to the Army and before doing so, 18 Command Workshop, REME at Bovington, spent three years carefully restoring it to full running order.

Mark IV Heavy Tank (Male)

Entered service: 1917
Crew: 8
Weight: 28,450kg/28 tons
Dimensions: Length – 8.03m/26ft 4in
   Height (over turret hatch) – 2.49m/8ft 2in
   Width – 3.91m/12ft 10in
Armament: Main – 2 x 6pdr (57mm/2.24in) guns
   Secondary – 4 x 7.7mm/0.303in Lewis
   machine-guns
Armour: Maximum – 12mm/0.47in
Powerplant: Daimler 6-cylinder petrol, developing
   74.57kW/100bhp
Performance: Speed – 6kph/3.7mph
   Range – 40km/25 miles

Mark V Heavy Tank

The major step forward achieved with the Mark V, designed in August 1917 and in the hands of troops in May 1918, was that one man could drive the tank by himself. This was because it was fitted with a four-speed epicyclic gearbox designed by W. G. Wilson, replacing the change-speed gearing of earlier models. The engine was a purpose-built Ricardo, developing 111.85kW/150hp. The tank also had better observation and ventilation, while the 273 litres/60 gallons of petrol contained in armoured fuel tanks at the tail gave a radius of action of 72.4km/45 miles compared with 38.6km/24 miles of the early Marks and 40km/25 miles of the Mark IV. A total of 200 Males and 200 Females were built between December 1917 and June 1918. One device that could be fitted to the Mark IV or Mark V was the Tadpole Tail – a device which lengthened the tank by about 2.74m/9ft to improve its performance. However, this lacked both rigidity and lateral stability.

The most ideal solution came with the Mark VA, when an additional 1.83m/6ft of armour was added between the sponson opening and the epicyclic gear housing, allowing additional storage space to carry up to 25 men. As a result, the weight went up from 29,465kg/29 tons to 33,530kg/ 33 tons and, because the engine power was not increased, the tank was much less manoeuvrable and slower than the standard Mark V.

TOP: **The Mark V Heavy Tank, which is in immaculate running order, belonging to the Tank Museum. The major advance with the Mark V was the fact that it could be driven by one man and thus did not require secondary gearsmen to change gear.** ABOVE: **A Mark V Heavy Tank demonstrates how the unditching beam is used – attached to the tracks by chains, tracks then rotate, bringing the beam down until it can get some purchase so as to assist in egress.**

Mark V Heavy Tank No. 9199, now at the Tank Museum and still in full running order, was issued to the 8th Battalion, Tank Corps, in July 1918. They were the first battalion to receive the Mark V. Crew H 41 were the first to see action in 9199, the commander, Lt H. A. Whittenbury, writing afterwards, "8th August 1918. Commenced the attack at 8:20am preceding the infantry by about 100yds ... enemy gun flashes observed ... Drove on zig-zag course ... Both six pounders had picked up targets and were firing ... Drove down steep slope into ravine ... opened fire with both six pounders firing HE and case shot at 40yds range into trenches and dugouts. Also fired a good many rounds with front Hotchkiss and observed many casualties."

At 10:15am, after a fierce battle, H 41 returned unscathed, having expended 87 6pdr HE, 18 case shot and 1,960 Hotchkiss rounds. Whittenbury would be awarded a Military Cross for his gallant action.

The following month, with a different commander, H 41 preceeded an infantry attack on the village of Estrees and was hit by shellfire which damaged its left track, but they managed to get back to the rallying point before the track broke.

From 1918–19 No. 9199 was used for training at Bovington, then in 1921 it went to the 4th Battalion, Tank Corps at Wogret Camp near Wareham until 1925, when it returned to Bovington. During World War II it was used for towing and recovery by the Camp Workshops and the Driving and Maintenance School, then in 1949 it was donated to the Tank Museum.

ABOVE: **Mark V Heavy Tank No. 9199 at the Bovington Tank Museum, painted in its World War I colours. The white/red/white stripes on the nose were British tank recognition markings that were still being used at the start of World War II in the Western Desert.** LEFT: **This Mark V has really got itself stuck in a very deep hole and will need more than an unditching beam to free itself!** BELOW: **The Mark V* had an additional 1.82m/6ft of armour added between the sponson housing and the epicyclic gear housing. Not only did this improve its trench-crossing ability, it also gave much more storage room inside (e.g. it could carry 25 men or the equivalent weight in stores).**

Mark V Heavy Tank (Male)

Entered service: 1918
Crew: 8
Weight: 29,465kg/29 tons
Dimensions: Length – 8.03m/26.4ft in
   Height (over turret hatch) – 2.49m/8ft 2in
   Width – 3.91m/12ft 10in
Armament: Main – 2 x 6pdr (57mm/2.24in) gun
   Secondary – 4 x 7.7mm/0.303in Hotchkiss machine-guns
Armour: Maximum – 12mm/0.47in
Powerplant: Ricardo 6-cylinder petrol, 111.85kW/150hp
Performance: Speed – 7.4kph/4.6mph
   Range – 72.4km/45 miles

Mark VI Light Tank

The Mark VI Light Tank was similar to the Mark V Light Tank, except for its turret which was redesigned to allow room for a wireless. This tank was produced in a number of versions, the main two being the Mark VIA and VIB. The Mark VIA had a single return roller removed from the top of the leading bogie and attached to the hull sides, and an octagonal cupola fitted with two lookouts.

The differences in the Mark VIB were to simplify production, and included a one-piece armoured louvre over the radiator (rather than two pieces) and a plain circular commander's cupola, replacing the faceted one of the Mark VIA, fitted with glass block lookouts.

The Light Tank Mk VI series entered production in 1936, and a thousand were in service worldwide with the British Army at the outbreak of World War II. In 1940, both in Europe and North Africa, the Light Mark VI formed a major part of the British tank strength. When the British Expeditionary Force (BEF) sailed for France in 1940, this tank was to be found in all divisional cavalry regiments and in the cavalry light tank regiments of 1st Armoured Division. Unfortunately, it was widely used in roles other than that for which it was designed (reconnaissance) and suffered heavy losses when used in a front-line role, especially when confronted by the better-armed and armoured German

TOP: **The immaculately restored Mark VIB Light Tank is in full running order at the Tank Museum, Bovington. It entered production in 1936, and over a thousand were in worldwide service when war began.** ABOVE: **Equipped with flotation gear, this Mark VI Light Tank carried out successful swimming trials.**

tanks. However, the Mark VI served with distinction not only in France, but in the Western Desert, Greece, Malta, Crete and Syria (with the Australians), and took part in the siege of Tobruk.

It was, however, woefully under-armoured (10mm/0.39in maximum armour thickness) and under-gunned (just machine-guns). In fact, some of the Light Mark VIs that were rushed

ABOVE: **Speeding across the training area at Bovington, Dorset, this Mark VIB Light Tank could reach a speed of 56kph/35mph on roads.** RIGHT: **The last of the series – the Mark VIC Light Tank had its Vickers machine-guns replaced by one 7.92mm/0.312in Besa and one 15mm/0.59in Besa air-cooled machine-gun. It also had wider suspension wheels and broader tracks.** BELOW: **Good photograph of a Vickers Mark VIA Light Tank. The commander wears the badge of the 3rd The King's Own Hussars who were part of 1st (Light) Armoured Brigade.**

over to France to support the BEF did not even have their machine-guns because they were still packed in grease in their crates on board ships that had yet to arrive! No wonder the commander of 1st Armoured Division, Maj Gen Roger Evans, would later write of it as: "this travesty of an armoured division". Thus, the tank crews had just their pistols as their tanks' only offensive weapons!

Mark VIB Light Tank	
Entered service: 1937	
Crew: 2	
Weight: 5,080kg/5 tons	
Dimensions: Length – 4.01m/13ft 2in	
Height (over turret hatch) – 2.26m/7ft 5in	
Width – 2.08m/6ft 10in	
Armament: Main – 1 x 12.7mm/0.5in or	
1 x 15mm/0.59in machine-gun	
Secondary – 1 x 7.7mm/0.303in Vickers or	
1 x 7.92mm/0.312in Besa machine-gun	
Armour: Maximum – 10mm/0.394in	
Powerplant: Meadows 6-cylinder, 65.6kW/88bhp	
Performance: Speed – 56kph/34.78mph	
Range – 200km/124.2 miles	

Mark VIII Heavy Tank

Instead of just improving on existing Marks, the Mark VIII Heavy Tank was an entirely new design. The "International", as it was called, was the largest, heaviest and most powerful of all the British World War I heavy tanks. It had a Ricardo V12 (or Liberty V12) engine, producing 223.7kW/300hp at 1,250rpm. At 37,593kg/37 tons it was a good 9,144kg/9 tons heavier than the Mark I, with roughly double the power-to-weight ratio. This was to have been a joint Anglo-American venture to build in all some 4,450 tanks "to win the war in 1919", along with 2,000 Mark Xs which never reached a full design stage.

Before the war ended, the British sent one of the few Mark VIIIs they had constructed over to the USA so that they could replicate it – although the Americans decided to fit their own Liberty V12 engine in place of the British Ricardo.

However, the Armistice rapidly put paid to their grandiose ideas and, although about 100 Mark VIIIs were built by the Americans after the war, only five were ever completed by

ABOVE: **Moving the Tank Museum's International. After spending many years outside in all weathers, the Mark VIII was moved under cover into the new "George Forty Hall", together with all the other priceless World War I exhibits, during the mid-1980s.** RIGHT: Cutaway drawing of the Mark VIII, showing its main components.

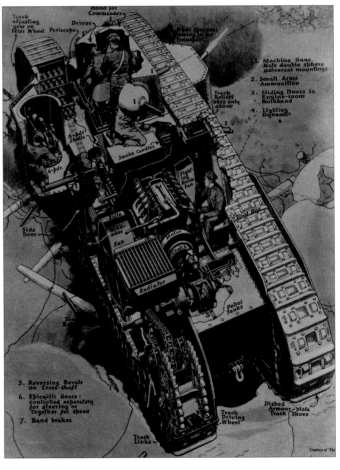

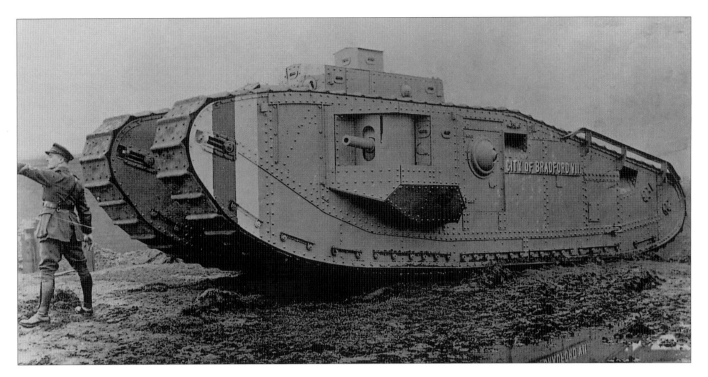

the British before the Armistice, and only three of these reached the troops. Armed with two 6pdrs, seven machine-guns, and a separate engine compartment (the first heavy tank to have one), it had great potential and would undoubtedly have been a battle-winner.

In 1940 the US Army sent some of the Mark VIIIs to Canada to help train the newly forming Canadian armoured units (they also sent a number of the Ford 6 Ton version of the Renault FT-17).

Not shown here, because it was a troop/cargo carrier rather than a tank, is the Mark IX, the very last British design of World War I to go into action. It had four large oval doors (two on each side) instead of gun sponsons, and could carry 10 tons of stores or 30 fully equipped infantrymen inside its capacious interior and thus under armour. One of its prototypes was even made amphibious by attaching large air drums to its sides, and was being tested on Armistice Day!

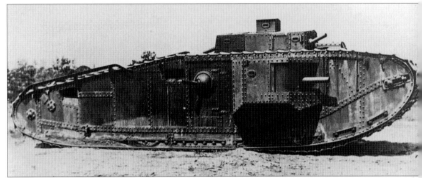

TOP, ABOVE AND BELOW: **This selection of all-round views of the Mark VIII give an excellent impression of the entirely new design of the International – so named because it was going to be built by Britain and the USA as a joint venture "to win the war in 1919". The Armistice put paid to that, with only some 100 of the proposed 4,500 being built. Only five were completed, and only three reached troops before the war ended.**

**Mark VIII
Heavy Tank**

Entered service: 1918
Crew: 8
Weight: 37,593kg/37 tons
Dimensions: Length – 10.41m/34ft 2in
    Height (over turret hatch) – 3.12m/10ft 3in
    Width – 3.76m/12ft 4in
Armament: Main – 2 x 6pdr (57mm/2.24in) guns
    Secondary – 7 x 7.7mm/0.303in machine-guns
Armour: Maximum – 16mm/0.63in
Powerplant: Ricardo or Liberty V12 petrol,
    223.7kW/300bhp
Performance: Speed – 9.7kph/6mph
    Range – 88km/55 miles

M1 and M2 Combat Cars

At the beginning of World War II, the United States had four closely related basic types of light AFV. The Infantry had Light Tanks M2A2 and M2A3, while the Cavalry, who were not allowed to have tanks, called theirs Combat Cars M1 and M2. The simplest way of telling them apart was that the light tanks had twin turrets, earning themselves the nickname of "Mae Wests" (for obvious anatomical reasons)!

The Combat Cars had single octagonal turrets with two machine-guns, one 12.7mm/0.5in and one 7.62mm/0.3in calibre, mounted coaxially. All had a second 7.62mm/ 0.3in machine-gun in the hull, and a third for anti-aircraft defence – the first recorded instance of this provision on any AFV.

Both the M1 and M2 had a crew of four, two in the turret and two in the hull. However, it must be said that both these vehicles were totally inadequate for operating on the modern battlefield of the time, except in a scouting role, and fortunately they never had to prove themselves in battle.

The Combat Car M2 was the first to be fitted with the distinctive trailing idler wheel, which increased the vehicle's footprint and aided traction and therefore

ABOVE LEFT: **What's in a name? These little light tanks were called Combat Cars because the US Cavalry were not allowed to have tanks!** ABOVE: **A company of M1 and M2 Combat Cars under a very special commander, Major Ernie Harmon, who would go on to become one of the US Army's star armoured battlefield commanders during World War II.**

overall performance. It also had its power plant changed from a Continental petrol engine to a Guiberson diesel radial engine. In 1940, with the formation of the American Armored Force, the need for the "Combat Car" subterfuge became unnecessary and Combat Cars M1 and M2 became known as the M1A1 and M1A2 Light Tanks.

ABOVE: **A close-up of M1 Combat Cars belonging to the 1st Cavalry Regiment. Here the commanders man their pintle-mounted anti-aircraft machine-guns with air-cooled barrels.**

M1 Combat Car	
Entered service: 1935	
Crew: 4	
Weight: 8,528kg/8.39 tons	
Dimensions: Length – 4.14m/13ft 7in	
Height (over turret hatch) – 2.36m/7ft 9in	
Width – 2.39m/7ft 10in	
Armament: Main – 12.7mm/0.5in machine-gun	
Secondary – 3 x 7.62mm/0.3in machine-guns	
Armour: Maximum – 16mm/0.63in	
Powerplant: Continental W-670 7-cylinder petrol, 186.4kW/250hp	
Performance: Speed – 72.4kph/45mph	
Range – 161km/100 miles	

LEFT: A "Mae West" (so called because it had twin turrets!) fords a stream during training. Note that no armament is installed. ABOVE: This M2A4, the very first US-built tank to arrive in the UK, is seen here being inspected by General (later Field Marshal) Alexander.

M2 Light Tank series

As World War II approached, the Americans still had four basic types of light armoured vehicle, all of which were closely related because all had been developed from the T2 tank series. The two infantry tanks were known as the M2A2 and M2A3. The M2A2 had numerous development models with a mixture of petrol and diesel engines, modified suspensions and other features. These were all of a similar size, weight, crew and armament, and all had twin turrets. The best was probably the M2A2E3, developed in 1938, which had a modified suspension with a trailing idler.

BELOW: An M2A2 Light Tank being driven up a loading ramp onto a rail flat car. One turret contains a 12.7mm/0.5inch machine-gun, the other a 7.62mm/0.30 inch machine-gun.

The M2A3 was an improved version of the M2A2, and appeared during 1938. Not only did it have slightly thicker frontal armour, better engine cooling and improved engine access, but it also had a longer track base, which necessitated repositioning the bogie units. Last of the development models of the M2A3s was the M2A3E3, which had a reworked suspension with a trailing idler wheel, giving it a better cross-country performance.

The M2A4 represented the last model of the M2 Light Tank series and was perhaps the most important and best of them all. For the first time it had a main armament larger than a machine-gun, the 37mm/1.46in M5 tank gun which had an armour-piercing capability. This was housed in a single turret with an all-round

manual traverse. One hundred and three rounds were carried on board for the gun which, even though it did not have much hitting power (it could only penetrate 25.4mm/1in of armour at 914m/1,000 yards), was just coming into service as the US Army's standard anti-tank gun.

The pilot model of the M2A4 was completed at Rock Island Arsenal in early 1939. The single turret had been found to be greatly superior to the twin "Mae Wests", while the tank had thicker armour on the front and hull sides (up to 25mm/0.98in), which increased the weight up to 12,193kg/12 tons and reduced its top speed accordingly. Nevertheless, the M2A4 was undoubtedly the best of the early American light tanks and would lead directly on to the M3 light – the famous Honey.

M2A4 Light Tank

Entered service: 1940
Crew: 4
Weight: 12,193k/12 tons
Dimensions: Length – 4.45m/14ft 7in
    Height (over turret hatch) – 2.52m/8ft 3in
    Width – 2.54m/8ft 4in
Armament: Main – 37mm/1.46m gun
    Secondary – 4 x 7.62mm/0.3in machine-guns
Armour: Maximum – 25mm/0.98in
Powerplant: Continental 7-cylinder radial, 186.6kW/250hp
Performance: Speed – 54.7kph/34mph
    Range – 209km/130 miles

M3 General Lee Medium Tank and variants

The British called the standard M3 the "General Lee", after the Civil War General Robert E. Lee. Its main armament was the sponson-mounted 75mm/2.95in gun which only had a limited traverse. In the fully rotating turret on the top of the tank was a 37mm/1.46in gun and coaxial machine-gun. There were up to three more machine-guns – one in the commander's cupola and either one or two fixed machine-guns firing through the front plate (the earlier production models had two).

M3 General Grant Medium Tank

The British version of the M3 was purchased under Lend-Lease by a special Tank Commission and modified for British Army service. It differed from the General Lee in having a larger turret with a bulge at the rear to take a radio set. This meant that the operator could also act as loader for the 37mm/1.46in gun, and one crew member fewer was needed to man the "General Grant", as the British version was called (after General

RIGHT: **A British-crewed M3 Medium Grant is admired by some local boys in Tunisia. The Grant had no commander's cupola, so it was lower. It also had a larger turret with room for the radio in the bustle.**

Ulysses S. Grant). The commander's cupola was also dispensed with, thus reducing the overall height by some 101mm/4in. The General Grant made a significant impact in the Western Desert and was later used in Europe and the Far East, where it did excellent work, "bunker-bashing" and supporting infantry.

The Lee had a seven-man crew – commander, 37mm/1.46in gunner, 37mm/1.46in loader, 75mm/2.95in

ABOVE: **The American M3 Medium Tank, known to the British as the "General Lee". It was then specially modified for British service, their model being known as the "General Grant". This Lee belongs to the Budge Collection and was taking part in an Open Day at the Tank Museum, Bovington. There is no commander's cupola on this particular M3 Lee.**

gunner, 75mm/2.95in loader, radio operator and driver. In the Grant, the 37mm/1.46in loader doubled up as a radio operator.

LEFT: **On show at the Bovington Tank Museum is this General Grant, as supplied to the British. It differs from the Lee by not having a commander's cupola, and with an enlarged turret bustle in the top turret for the wireless, thus saving one crewman.**

ABOVE: **This shows a T5 Phase III Medium Tank, photographed at the Rock Island arsenal in 1938. It was the prototype of the standard M2 Medium Tank and the forerunner of the M3.**
ABOVE RIGHT: **This M3A1 is a Lee with the additional commander's cupola and a cast hull. Later production models had no side door or escape hatch in the floor.** RIGHT: **This is the M3A2, again a Lee, but with an all-welded hull.**

M3 in combat

The first M3s to see action were those sent with British Eighth Army in the Western Desert in 1942. Rommel wrote in his diary of them: "The advent of the new American tank has torn great holes in our ranks. Our entire force now stood in heavy and destructive combat with a superior enemy."

M3 Grant Canal Defence Light

When the M3 was replaced by the Sherman M4, a number of British Grants were fitted with a Canal Defence Light similar to that which had been previously installed in the Matilda CDL. The turret was removed and replaced with an armoured searchlight housing, sporting a dummy wooden gun, but also containing a machine-gun.

M3 General Grant Medium Tank

Entered service: 1941
Crew: 6 (7 on the Lee)
Weight: 27,219kg/26.7 tons
Dimensions: Length – 5.64m/18ft 6in
    Height (over turret hatch) – 3.12m/10ft 3in
    Width – 2.72m/8ft 11in
Armament: Main – 75mm/2.95in M2 or M3 gun
    Secondary – 37mm/1.46in M5 or M6 cannon,
    4 x 7.62mm/0.3in machine-guns
Armour: Maximum – 57mm/2.24in
Powerplant: Continental R-975-EC2 radial petrol,
    253.5kW/340hp
Performance: Speed – 42kph/26mph
    Range – 193km/120 miles

M4 Sherman Medium Tank

Of all the tanks ever built, the M4 Sherman was undoubtedly the most widely used by all the Allies, a staggering 49,234 Sherman guns tanks being produced in the USA, more than half the entire American wartime tank production and equal to the total combined wartime output of Great Britain and Germany! Add to this the vast number of variants and the figure becomes even more impressive.

The M4 Medium was the logical successor to the M3 Medium Tank Lee/Grant, and about the same time as the latter was first going into production, the Ordnance Committee directed that work should begin on its successor because they appreciated that the M3 was only a stopgap. This resulted in the construction of the Medium Tank T6 (the prototype M4) at the Aberdeen Proving Ground in early 1941. Clearly there was British and Canadian input into the design, which bore a striking resemblance to the Canadian Ram Medium Tank.

At about the same time, the Rock Island Arsenal built a second pilot model and, in September 1941, the new tank was quickly standardized, entering service on September 5, 1941, as the Medium Tank M4. Interestingly, one of the new tank factories to build the Sherman had first to be built from scratch near Detroit – in just three months from breaking earth to rolling out the first tank! Full-scale production would end in early 1944, by which time six basic models of the gun tank, designated M4 through to M4A6 (less M4A5), had been built.

The Sherman, as it was soon called, would first see active service with the British 8th Army in North Africa in October 1942. Two months later, it was first used in action by American troops in Tunisia in early December 1942. The M4 was an extremely robust and reliable tank which used the same basic chassis as the M3 Medium; it therefore had vertical volute spring suspension, a rear engine and front drive. There were six

TOP: **The Canadian-built "Grizzly I" is virtually identical to the M4 Sherman, apart from having different drive sprockets and tracks. Nearly 50,000 Shermans were built during World War II.** ABOVE: **This immaculate Sherman M4A1E8 (76) is privately owned by the Indiana Military Museum in Vincennes, USA. The "Easy Eight" had an improved suspension and mounted the 76mm/2.99in gun.**

basic Marks of Sherman produced in three main tank factories in the USA. Initially armed with the 75mm/2.95in gun, there were also two models with close-support 105mm/4.13in howitzers, four with the improved 76mm/2.99in gun and "Wet" stowage (ammunition in water-protected racks below the turret) and, finally, a heavily armoured assault version nicknamed "Jumbo".

The main change from the M3 Medium was the fact that Sherman had a fully rotating turret instead of its main gun being in a side sponson. Not only did this give the gun all-round traverse, but also meant that the crew could be reduced to five: three in the turret (commander, gunner and loader/operator) and two in the hull (driver and co-driver/hull gunner). The Sherman was a very user-friendly AFV, and well able to deal with most terrain. Unfortunately, however, it had a tendency to catch fire easily when struck by enemy shells – the Allies nicknamed it the "Ronson Lighter" because it was guaranteed to light first time, while the Germans called it the "Tommy Cooker" – hence the wet stowage arrangement when the tank was re-gunned, plus the addition of appliqué armour and even sandbags, to increase protection. A continuing shortage of the initial R-975 Continental air-cooled radial aircraft engine led to the forced adoption of no fewer than four further engines, both petrol and diesel, including the remarkable Chrysler multi-bank 30-cylinder petrol engine.

The Sherman was adapted to perform a wide range of specialized tasks with conversion to swimming tanks (the addition of a flotation screen in the highly secret Sherman DD swimming tank, used most effectively during the D-Day landings), engineer/dozer vehicles, tank recovery vehicles, beach recovery vehicles, armoured personnel carriers, assault bridge-carriers, flamethrower tanks, mine-clearing tanks (including flails, rollers and explosives – even a mine-resistant vehicle), self-propelled guns, howitzer, anti-aircraft gun and rocket platforms, and as tank destroyers to name but a few! The British had their own designations for the wide range of variants, which included the most effective Sherman to see wartime action – the Firefly, which mounted a highly effective 17pdr gun.

The Sherman's versatility was immense and did not end when war finished. After 1945, the Sherman was used by many armies worldwide, especially by the Israelis who, in their own inimitable way, adapted the tank for a wide variety of uses and prolonged its life as a gun tank by refitting with improved engine, main armament and armour.

ABOVE: **This massive rocket array, mounted on top of a sandbagged Sherman, was known as the Rocket Launcher T 34 "Calliope". It consisted of 60 x 117mm/4.6in rocket tubes and saw limited combat during World War II.**
BELOW: **US Marines hitch a ride. Tank-borne infantry moving up to occupy Ghuta on Okinawa. There are at least 18 "passengers" hitching a ride, which is fine until the tank has to use its guns.**

RIGHT: **A Sherman fords a canal near Nancy, France, September 12, 1944. Note the foliage cut as camouflage to break up the tank's unmistakable outline, and also the heavy 12.7mm/0.5in Browning Heavy AA machine-gun on top of the turret.**

M4 Sherman Medium Tank (mid-production)

Entered service: 1941
Crew: 5
Weight: 30,339kg/29.86 tons
Dimensions: Length – 5.88m/19ft 4in
  Height (over turret hatch) – 2.74m/ 9ft
  Width – 2.68m/8ft 10in
Armament: Main – 75mm/2.95in M3 gun
  Secondary – 2 x 7.62in/0.3in and
  1 x 12.7mm/0.5in AA (anti-aircraft) machine-guns
Armour: Maximum – 75mm/2.95in
Powerplant: Continental R-975C1 Petrol, 9-cylinder
  4-cycle radial, 298.5kW/400hp
Performance: Speed – 39kph/24.2mph
  Range – 192km/119.3 miles

M3 Light Tank series

The M2A4 was effectively a prototype for the next light tank, the M3, which had many of its features, such as the single rotating seven-sided turret and 37mm/1.46in gun. The M3 was designed in the spring of 1940, the main requirement being for thicker armour which increased the weight to 12,904kg/12.7 tons combat-loaded, and required stronger suspension. Nicknamed the Honey, the M3 first saw action with the British Army in the Western Desert, where it was officially known as the Stuart I in British Army nomenclature.

The first production models of the M3 were of a riveted construction, but they were soon followed in the series with increasing proportions with welded armour. There were also petrol and diesel engine variants. With the M3A1, the side sponson machine-guns were soon removed because they could not be properly aimed and must have wasted a great deal of ammunition. There was also now no commander's cupola; instead the turret had a basket and a power traverse.

The final model of the M3 series was the M3A3 (Stuart V in British parlance). It had a larger turret and no side sponsons, which created space for extra fuel tanks and ammunition stowage. An experimental model, which had twin Cadillac engines, a turret basket and other modifications, was the prototype for the M5 Light Tank.

ABOVE: **The M3A1 Light Tank was so well liked by its crews that they called it the Honey when it first came into British service in the Western Desert in 1941. Their experience led to modifications such as the removal of the two sponson machine-guns.**

M3A1 Light Tank Stuart Mk III

Entered service: 1940
Crew: 4
Weight: 12,904kg/12.7 tons
Dimensions: Length – 4.52m/14ft 10in
　　Height (over turret hatch) – 2.31m/7ft 7in
　　Width – 2.24m/7ft 4in
Armament: Main – 37mm/1.46in M6 gun
　　Secondary – 3 x 7.62mm/0.3in machine-guns
Armour: Maximum – 51mm/2.01in
Powerplant: Continental W-670, 7-cylinder radial petrol, 186.4kW/250hp
Performance: Speed – 58kph/36mph
　　Range – 113km/70 miles

M5 Light Tank

ABOVE: **The end of the Honey tank line was the M5 that came off the assembly line in March 1942. This beautifully restored M5A1 belongs to Judge Jim Osborne of the Indiana Military Museum, Vincennes, Indiana.**

The end of the Honey line was the M5 – they missed out the "M4" designation so as not to cause confusion with the M4 Sherman. It shared the same weapon systems as the M3, and first came off the assembly line in March 1942, with the British calling it the Stuart VI. It weighed 14,936kg/14.7 tons and was powered by two Cadillac engines, giving the vehicle a top speed of 60kph/37mph.

M5 Light Tank

Entered service: 1942
Crew: 4
Weight: 14,936kg/14.7 tons
Dimensions: Length – 4.34m/14ft 3in
　　Height (over turret hatch) – 2.31m/7ft 7in
　　Width – 2.26m/7ft 5in
Armament: Main – 37mm/1.46in M6 gun
　　Secondary – 3 x 7.62mm/0.3in machine-guns
Armour: Maximum – 64mm/2.52in
Powerplant: 2 x Cadillac Series 42 V8, each developing 82kW/110hp
Performance: Speed – 60kph/37mph
　　Range – 161km/100 miles

M6 Heavy Tank

Until the start of World War II the USA had shown little interest in heavy tanks, one major reason being the difficulty of transporting them, especially overseas. However, the success of German armour and the obvious vulnerability and lack of firepower of the standard light and medium tanks led to a recommendation to develop a heavy tank in the 50,800kg/50-ton class.

Designed in 1940, the M6 Heavy Tank weighed almost 45 tons and was armed with a 76.2mm/3in main gun, plus a 37mm/1.46in gun mounted coaxially, and a total of four machine-guns (two 12.7mm/0.5in and two 7.62mm/0.3in). Its armour was up to 133mm/5.24in thick and it had a top speed of 35kph/22mph. When it appeared in 1942 it was the most powerful tank in the world.

However, the Armored Force were not impressed with the new tank and, after testing, concluded that it was too heavy, did not have a large enough main armament and suffered from transmission problems. Some 40 vehicles were built, but they were only ever used for trial purposes.

LEFT: **This M6A2 Heavy Tank weighed 45,316kg/44.6 tons and was armed with a 76.2mm/3in gun. Originally designed as the heavy counterpart to the M3/M4 Mediums, only 40 were ever built of all models, and it never saw operational service.**

M6 Heavy Tank

Entered service: 1942
Crew: 5
Weight: 45,316kg/44.6 tons
Dimensions: Length – 8.43m/27ft 8in
  Height (over turret hatch) – 3.23m/10ft 7in
  Width – 3.23m/10ft 7in
Armament: Main – 1 x 76.2mm/3in gun and
  1 x 37mm/1.46in gun
  Secondary – 2 x 12.7mm/0.5in and
  2 x 7.62mm/0.3in machine-guns
Armour: Maximum – 133mm/5.24in
Powerplant: Wright Whirlwind G-200 9-cylinder
  radial, 690kW/925hp
Performance: Speed – 35kph/22mph
  Range – 161km/100 miles

M26 Pershing Heavy Tank

The M26 Pershing was developed from the T26 series – the outcome of reclassifying the T25 as a heavy tank in June 1944. Weighing about 41 tons, with a 90mm/3.54in main gun, 102.6mm/4in armour on the front of the turret and a top speed of 48kph/30mph, the new tank was just about a match for the German Tiger I, produced some years earlier. There were also attempts to further upgrade the main armament, such as the T15E1 gun, and to increase the armour by welding extra plates on the front of the hull. It was the most powerful American tank to see combat in World War II. Wartime production of the M26 totalled 1,436. It went on to see service in the Korean War.

M26 Pershing Heavy Tank

Entered service: 1944
Crew: 5
Weight: 41,861kg/41.2 tons
Dimensions: Length – 8.61m/28ft 3in
  Height (over turret hatch) – 2.77m/9ft 1in
  Width – 3.51m/11ft 6in
Armament: Main – 90mm/3.54in M3 gun
  Secondary – 1 x 12.7mm/0.5in and
  2 x 7.62mm/0.31in machine-guns
Armour: Maximum – 102.6mm/4in
Powerplant: Ford GAF, 373kW/500hp
Performance: Speed – 48kph/30mph
  Range – 161km/100 miles

LEFT: **The M26 Pershing was the most powerful and best all-round American tank of World War II, but was only standardized and entered service in 1944. Its 90mm/3.54in main gun was almost on a par with the German 8.8cm/3.46in. It went on to do well following World War II, seeing service in the Korean War (1950–53).**

M10 Wolverine Tank Destroyer

This was the first really successful tank destroyer in the US Army. With a five-sided open topped turret it had a crew of five, a 76mm/2.99in main gun and could carry 54 rounds of ammunition. It had a top speed of 48kph/30mph and weighed 29,059kg/28.6 tons – with a counterweight needed to the rear of the turret to balance the gun. A total of 5,000 M10s were built between September 1942 and December 1943, initially using the Lee/Grant M3 standard chassis, then the M4 Sherman chassis.

ABOVE: **The M10 Wolverine was a well-liked and effective American tank destroyer, armed with a 76mm/2.99in M7 gun. The M10 was based on the M3 medium chassis, and the M10A1 was based on the M4 Sherman.**

M10 Achilles Tank Destroyer

The British up-gunned some of the M10s they received from America by fitting their highly lethal 17pdr. The result was known as "Achilles", with a similar open-topped turret to Wolverine and its counter-weight situated at the end of the gun barrel

M10 Wolverine TD	
Entered service: 1942	
Crew: 5	
Weight: 29,059kg/28.6 tons	
Dimensions: Length – 5.82m/19ft 1in	
Height (over turret hatch) – 2.49m/8ft 2in	
Width – 3.05m/10ft	
Armament: Main – 76mm/2.99in M7 gun	
Secondary – 12.7mm/0.5in machine-gun	
Armour: Maximum – 37mm/1.46in	
Powerplant: 2 x GMS6-71 diesel	
Performance: Speed 48kph/30mph	
Range – 322km/200 miles	

just behind the muzzle brake. Fast and hard-hitting, it was one of the best Allied tank killers of World War II.

LEFT: **Most effective of the M10s was the British conversion, known as "Achilles", which mounted the Ordnance quick-firing 17pdr Mark 5 in place of the 76mm/2.99in gun. This was the same gun as mounted on the Sherman Firefly and the Challenger A30.**

LEFT: **The M18 Hellcat was well liked by its crews and it knocked out many enemy AFVs in north-west Europe and Italy, where it was widely used. It was light (18,187kg/17.9 tons) and fast, and it carried a lethal punch with its 76mm/2.99in M1 gun. It also had an excellent cross-country performance and a good turn of speed. The 76mm/2.99in gun (as fitted in later Shermans) had a maximum range of 14,721m/16,100yds and used APCBC/HE-T.**

M18 Hellcat Tank Destroyer

The Hellcat was also very fast, with a top speed of 80–89kph/50–55mph. Its lower silhouette from a redesigned turret and good cross-country performance made it liked by its crews and an excellent hit-and-run hunter-killer. Similar to the Wolverine, it mounted a 76mm/2.99in main gun and a 12.7mm/0.5in machine-gun for close defence.

M18 Hellcat TD

Entered service: 1943
Crew: 5
Weight: 18,187kg/17.9 tons
Dimensions: Length – 6.66m/21ft 10in
  Height (over turret hatch) – 2.57m/8ft 5in
  Width – 2.97m/9ft 9in
Armament: Main – 76mm/2.99in M1 gun
  Secondary – 12.7mm/0.5in machine-gun
Armour: Maximum – 12mm/0.47in
Powerplant: Continental R-975, 9-cylinder radial, 298.5kW/400hp
Performance: Speed – 89kph/55mph
  Range – 241km/150 miles

M36 Gun Motor Carriage

Most effective of all American tank destroyers was the M36, which mounted a 90mm/3.54in main gun that was the most powerful on the battlefield to date. The only problem was the weight of the new gun which necessitated the creation of a new rounded turret. Standardized in July 1944, the first of these new TDs arrived in Europe in August 1944 and were immediately in action.

Demand for the M36 Gun Motor Carriage increased enormously after the battles in Normandy which had shown that this was the best US weapon to deal with enemy tanks.

M36 Gun Motor Carriage

Entered service: 1944
Crew: 5
Weight: 28,145kg/27.7 tons
Dimensions: Length – 6.15m/20ft 2in
  Height (over turret hatch) – 2.72m/8ft 11 in
  Width – 3.05m/10ft
Armament: Main – 90mm/3.54in M3 gun
  Secondary – 12.7mm/0.5in machine-gun
Armour: Maximum – 50mm/1.97in
Powerplant: Ford GAA V8, 373kW/500hp
Performance: Speed – 48kph/30mph
  Range – 241km/150 miles

RIGHT: **The M36 Gun Motor Carriage mounted a 90mm/3.54in gun in an attempt to be able to knock out the large, better-armed enemy tanks such as Tiger and Panther. Over 1,500 were built and reached north-west Europe in September 1944.**

M22 Locust Light Tank

LEFT: Out of a total of just over 800 Locusts, the British took delivery of several hundred, issuing them to the 6th Airborne Armoured Reconnaissance Regiment to supplement the Tetrarchs carried in Hamilcar gliders. They saw action during the Rhine Crossing in March 1945. One M22 was rebuilt as the T10 Light Tractor (airborne) designed to carry five men, but this project was suspended in 1943.

M22 Locust Light Tank

Entered service: 1941
Crew: 3
Weight: 7,417kg/7.3 tons
Dimensions: Length – 3.94m/12ft 11in
Height (over turret hatch) – 1.73m/5ft 8in
Width – 2.24m/7ft 4in
Armament: Main – 37mm/1.46in M6 gun
Secondary – 7.62mm/0.3in machine-gun
Armour: Maximum – 25mm/0.98in
Powerplant: Lycoming 0-435T 6-cylinder radial, 121kW/162hp
Performance: Speed – 64kph/40mph
Range – 217km/135 miles

Designed as an airborne tank in 1941 by the charismatic J. Walter Christie, the M22 Locust only saw operational service with the British Army, who deployed it in small numbers with the 6th Airborne Reconnaissance Regiment during the Rhine Crossing. The Locust was transported by a Hamilcar glider, which had been specially designed to carry the British light airborne tank, the Tetrarch. The Locust was armed with a 37mm/1.46in gun and a coaxial machine-gun but it really proved too light to be of any great consequence on the battlefield.

M24 Chaffee Light Tank

Undoubtedly the best light tank of World War II was the M24 Chaffee, named after General Adna Chaffee, the "Father of the US Armored Force". It was a five-man tank, but was normally manned by only four men due to manpower shortages. The main armament was a powerful 75mm/2.95in gun which had been adapted from the heavy aircraft cannon as used in the B-25G Mitchell bomber. Although no match for the bigger German tanks, the M24 was remarkably effective against smaller targets. It remained the standard US light tank long after the end of the war and was modified to anti-aircraft and mortar carriage variants. The M24 Chaffee also saw service in Korea in the 1950s.

M24 Chaffee Light Tank

Entered service: 1944
Crew: 4 or 5
Weight: 18,289kg/18 tons
Dimensions: Length – 5.49m/18ft
Height (over turret hatch) – 2.46m/8ft 1in
Width – 2.95m/9ft 8in
Armament: Main – 75mm/2.95in M6 gun
Secondary – 1 x 12.7mm/0.5in and 2 x 7.62mm/0.3in machine-guns
Armour: Maximum – 38mm/1.5in
Powerplant: 2 x Cadillac 44T24 V8, each developing 82kW/110hp
Performance: Speed – 55kph/34mph
Range – 282km/175 miles

LEFT: Named after the "Father" of the Armored Force, General Adna R. Chaffee, the M24 was not a great success as a gun tank either during World War II or in the early part of the Korean War, when it was outgunned by the North Korean T-34/85. Variants included the M19 GMC, an AA tank mounting twin 40mm/1.58in guns, and the M41 HMC, mounting a 155mm/6.1in M1 howitzer.

M1931 Christie

Tank development between the wars owed much to the brilliant, but unpredictable American engineer J. Walter Christie, who was the advocate of light, fast tanks that could move cross country at amazing speeds on his unique suspension system, or equally well without their tracks, just on their road wheels. His designs proved very influential in the burgeoning world of armour design beyond his native country, but closer to home in the USA he was regarded as a difficult man to deal with.

Based on his M1928 vehicle, the M1931 was modified to include a turret as well as various automotive improvements so that it was reputed to have had a top speed on its tracks of 74kph/46mph, while on its wheels on roads it could supposedly reach 113kph/70mph.

Although the US Army did not adopt his designs to a significant extent, other countries showed far more interest. Two of these tanks were purchased by the Russians and became the models for the BT series, while in the UK it was to influence British Cruiser tank development.

LEFT: **This is another of Christie's modern, streamlined tanks – the M1936 Airborne tank. Christie and his son are inside. Despite lack of interest in the USA, his revolutionary suspension was adopted by the British, the Poles and, most importantly, by the Soviet Union in their BT series.**

TOP: **Designed by the brilliant but irascible J. Walter Christie, the T3 Medium Tank was also called the Convertible and the 1928 Tank. It led on to the M1931 Medium Tank, which had a turret with a 37mm/1.46in gun.**
ABOVE: **The M1931 tank could run on its tracks, as seen here, or on its wheels.**

M1931 Christie

Entered service: 1931 (prototype only)
Crew: 2
Weight: 10,668kg/10.5 tons
Dimensions: Length – 5.43m/17ft 10in
   Height (over turret hatch) – 2.21m/7ft 3in
   Width – 2.24m/7ft 4in
Armament: Main – 37mm/1.46in gun
   Secondary – 7.62mm/0.3in machine-gun
Armour: Maximum – 16mm/0.63in
Powerplant: Liberty, 12-cylinder petrol, 252kW/338hp
Performance: Speed – 64kph/40mph (tracks),
   113kph/70mph (wheels)
   Range – 274km/170 miles

Neubaufahrzeuge V and VI

Tank production developed very rapidly in pre-World War II Nazi Germany. In addition to light and medium tanks, some interest was also shown in designing a heavy tank to follow on from the Grosstraktor. This new vehicle was simply called *Neubaufahrzeuge* (NbFz)

(New Construction Vehicle) and weighed about 24,385kg/24 tons. Five prototypes were built by Krupp and Rheinmetall, the former building the Model A, armed with coaxial 7.5cm/2.95in and 3.7cm/1.46in

guns, and the latter the Model B, mounting a 10.5cm/4.13in howitzer and a 3.7cm/1.46in gun. Both Models also had a second subsidiary turret in front of the main one, mounting two coaxial 7.62mm/0.3in machine-guns.

Ordered in 1934–35, the tanks were originally designated PzKpfw V and VI, but, as neither was put into production, these designations were passed on to the Panther and Tiger tanks. The prototype NbFzs were initially located at the tank training school at Putlos until early in 1940, when three were used in Norway. One was destroyed there and the other two returned to Germany towards the end of that year, where they returned to the panzer training school to be used as parade ornaments in the camp.

ABOVE AND BELOW LEFT: **As a direct result of the experience gained from the *Grosstraktor* (cover name for a heavy tank secretly produced in the late 1920s), Krupp and Rheinmetall were each asked to produce prototype heavy tanks *Neubaufahrzeuge* (New Construction Vehicle) Model A (NbFz VI) and Model B (NbFz V) respectively. Both were multi-turreted. Three were sent to Oslo, Norway, in April 1940 and saw action there, one being destroyed and the other two returning to Germany.**

Neubaufahrzeuge V/VI

Entered service: 1934
Crew: 6
Weight: 24,385kg/24 tons
Dimensions: Length – 7.32m/24ft
   Height (over turret hatch) – 2.72m/8ft 11in
   Width – 3.05m/10ft
Armament: Main – 7.5cm/2.95in gun or 10.5cm/4.13in howitzer and 1 x 3.7cm/1.46in coaxial gun
   Secondary – 3 x 7.92mm/0.312in machine-guns (2 x coaxial in subsidiary turret)
Armour: Maximum – 70mm/2.76in
Powerplant: 6-cylinder petrol, 372.9kW/500hp
Performance: Speed – 35.4kph/22mph
   Range – 140km/87 miles

PzKpfw Maus Super-Heavy Tank

Hitler's obsession with heavy tanks reached its zenith with the production of the super-heavies, of which only two models were actually ever built – Maus and the E-100 – although a number of others were talked about and some even reached the design stage. Clearly certain influential members of the German armaments industry shared Hitler's enthusiasm for super-heavy tanks, initially anyway, and foremost among them was Dr Porsche.

What is clear is that the time and energy spent on designing and producing these behemoths wasted a vast amount of precious design and production effort, which Germany could ill afford to spare. Guderian described the Maus as "this gigantic offspring of the fantasy of Hitler and his advisers" which originally started life under the more appropriate codename of *Mammut* (Mammoth).

The heaviest tank ever built, Maus weighed an incredible 191,000kg/188 tons – too heavy to cross any bridge or move anywhere off level ground on its own. Only one Maus was completed to the stage where it had a turret and armament, consisting of one 12.8cm/5.04in L/55 gun and one coaxial 7.5cm/2.95in L/36.5 gun. It is now in the Russian Tank Museum.

ABOVE AND BELOW LEFT: **Super-Heavy German Tank, Maus, which at 191,000kg/188 tons was the largest and heaviest tank ever built during World War II. It was designed to out-gun and outperform all Allied AFVs. With a 12.8cm/5.04in gun and immensely thick frontal armour, two prototypes were constructed in late 1943, but although five more were ordered, they were never completed. Maus did at least have its turret fitted, unlike E100. The tank is crammed with complicated machinery so it would have been difficult to maintain. It was intended to be submersible to a depth of 8m/26ft!**

PzKpfw Maus Super-Heavy Tank

Entered service: 1945 (prototype only)
Crew: 5
Weight: Approximately 191,000kg/188 tons
Dimensions: Length – 10.09m/33ft 1in
    Height (over turret hatch) – 3.66m/12ft
    Width – 3.67m/12ft 0.5in
Armament: Main – 12.8cm/5.04in and
    7.5cm/2.95in coaxial gun
    Secondary – 7.92mm/0.312in machine-gun
Armour: Maximum – 200mm/7.87in
Powerplant: Mercedes-Benz MB509 V12 petrol,
    783kW/1,080hp
Performance: Speed – 20kph/12.4mph
    Range – 186km/115.6 miles

PzKpfw I Light Tank

The PzKpfw I Ausf A was the first German tank to go into mass production. It had the same hull and suspension as its predecessor, the PzKpfw I Ausf A *Ohne Aufbau* (literally "without turret") which had been produced without a turret and weapon system to bypass the Treaty of Versailles that prevented Germany from building tanks. Weighing just over 5 tons, with a crew of two and mounting two 7.92mm/ 0.312in machine-guns, it was soon outclassed on the battlefield and was withdrawn from active service in 1941. The Ausf B had a slightly longer chassis than the Ausf A (just under 0.5m/8in longer) and a more powerful engine.

The modification increased its weight to 5,893kg/5.8 tons. It was also phased out of service in 1941.

There was also a command version of the PzKpfw I, which was used at company, battalion, regimental and brigade level in the headquarters of panzer units from the mid-1930s up to the early war years. A radio transmitter was included in addition to the radio receiver normally only fitted in the PzKpfw I. The superstructure had to be raised in height to make room for the radio and its operator.

Some versions of the Ausf B had an odd-looking cable-operated arm which could drop a demolition charge over the

ABOVE: **The PzKpfw I Ausf B was the second production model and entered service in 1935, being slightly longer than the Ausf A. It was armed with two machine-guns.** BELOW LEFT: **The Tank Museum's Kleinerbefelswagen I, the command version of the PzKpfw IB. It has a fixed turret and was for use by unit commanders.**

rear end of the tank. This could be placed near obstacles and then set off remotely.

The final development of the PzKpfw I was a 21,337kg/21-ton infantry assault tank, which had very thick armour. Thirty were built in 1942, and a few were taken to Russia for combat testing. However, as a result of these tests, further orders were cancelled.

PzKpfw I Ausf B Light Tank

Entered service: 1934
Crew: 2
Weight: 5,893kg/5.8 tons
Dimensions: Length – 4.42m/14ft 6in
  Height (over turret hatch) – 1.72m/5ft 8in
  Width – 2.06m/6ft 9in
Armament: Main – 2 x 7.92mm/0.312in machine-guns
Armour: Maximum – 13mm/0.51in
Powerplant: Maybach NL38TR, 6-cylinder petrol, 74.5kW/100hp
Performance: Speed – 40kph/24.9mph
  Range – 153km/95.1 miles

PzKpfw II Light Tank

The next model in the German light tank family was the PzKpfw II, weighing nearly 10 tons, with a crew of three, mounting a 2cm/0.79in cannon capable of firing both high-explosive and armour-piercing ammunition, along with a coaxial MG34 machine-gun. First manufactured in 1936, it underwent an initial development cycle of three versions – A, B and C, by which time the suspension had changed from one very similar to the PzKpfw I to five independently sprung, larger roadwheels and four top rollers. The A version is distinguishable from later models by the periscope on the turret top placed centrally behind the guns. With the B and C models only minor variations were made, which included extra bolted-on armour plate, improvements in vision devices and the addition of a turret cupola.

The PzKpfw II series then continued up to the Ausf L, with its armament remaining the same but with constant changes to its chassis, superstructure and automotive systems, as well as increases in armour thickness. PzKpfw IIs

saw action in all theatres and were later modified into a number of variants, including having the turret removed to become an artillery and ammunition "Schlepper". There was also the "Flamingo" flamethrower variant, which had two flamethrowers mounted on the front corners of the tank's superstructure.

The final model of this series was the Panzerspahwagen II Light Recce tank, called the *Luchs* (Lynx) and was

ABOVE: **PzKpfw II Ausf F. This was the final model of the normal PzKpfw II series. The major difference was that the hull was made from one flat 35mm/ 1.38in plate.**

designed and developed as a reconnaissance tank. It had a crew of four and weighed 13,208kg/13 tons. Its main armament was a 2cm/0.79in KwK38 gun, with a coaxially mounted MG34. About 100 were built in late 1943 and saw service in both Russia and Europe.

BELOW: **PzKpfw II Ausf L was also known as the *Luchs*. It was a light reconnaissance tank with a crew of four and weighed 13,208kg/13 tons. This one is in the Tank Museum, Bovington.**

PzKpfw II Ausf F Light Tank

Entered service: 1935 (Ausf A), 1941 (Ausf F)
Crew: 3
Weight: 9,650kg/9.5 tons
Dimensions: Length – 4.81m/15ft 9in
   Height (over turret hatch) – 2.15m/7ft 0.5in
   Width – 2.28m/7ft 8in
Armament: Main – 2cm/0.79in cannon
   Secondary – 7.92mm/0.315in machine-gun
Armour: Maximum – 35mm/1.38in
Powerplant: Maybach HL62TR, 6-cylinder petrol, 104.4kW/140hp
Performance: Speed – 40kph/24.9mph
   Range – 200km/124.3 miles

PzKpfw III Medium Tank

The backbone of the German Panzer Divisions was their medium tanks in the 15,240–20,320kg/15–20-ton range. Tracing its original development as far back as 1935, the PzKpfw III was a vital tank produced up until 1943. There were versions ranging from Ausf A–N (minus I and K), but with other variants including flamethrower, submersible, various command versions, and a turret-less ammunition carrier. The chassis was also the foundation of the StuG assault-gun series.

The early models mounted a KwK 3.7cm/1.46in gun, plus twin machine-guns in the turret and a third in the hull, manned by the radio operator. Ausf As were issued first in 1937, but withdrawn from service in early 1940 because their armour thickness, at only 15mm/0.59in, was found to be inadequate. By the time of the Ausf E, the tank still mounted the same armament, but its armour was now up to 30mm/1.18in and its weight had increased accordingly to over 19 tons.

The first model to mount the new KwK 5cm/1.97in gun (necessitating a turret redesign) was the Ausf F. First ordered in 1939, it saw service in Poland and France, when it was quickly realized that more armour and bigger guns were needed. The problem with the PzKpfw III was that it could not accept a gun larger than 5cm/1.97in because of the restrictive size of the turret ring. Six hundred Ausf G models were produced from April 1940 onwards, with their weight now just over 20,320kg/ 20 tons.

The Ausf L mounted the 5cm/1.97in KwK39 L/60 gun and once again had thicker armour on the front of the turret, now 57mm/2.24in. Ausf M came fitted with *Schürzen* (skirts) to protect from HEAT (High-Explosive Anti-Tank) weapons such as the bazooka and the PIAT.

TOP: **The Tank Museum's PzKpfw III Ausf L, which mounts a long-barrelled 5cm/1.97in KwK39 L/60 gun, the second model to do so. The Ausf L first saw action in USSR in 1942.** LEFT: **The Tank Museum's PzKpfw III going through its paces during a Tankfest. As can be seen, it is still in excellent running order.**

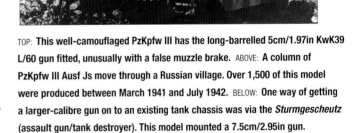

Variants included: a specially designed artillery OP tank (*Artillerie Panzerbeobachtungwagen*) to enable the Forward Observation Officer to accompany a panzer formation (the turret space normally taken up by the main armament being replaced by an artillery plotting board and extra radios); a command tank (*Panzerbefelswagen*); an armoured recovery vehicle (*Bergepanzer III*); a supply carrier (*Schlepper III*); and an engineer vehicle (*Pionerpanzer*). However, more remarkable was the *Tauchpanzer* (literally "diving tank") which was completely waterproofed so that it could operate at depths of 15m/50ft and remain submerged for up to 20 minutes. Designed for use in 1940 for the aborted invasion of England, they were later used to great effect for the crossing of the River Bug on June 22, 1941, at the start of the invasion of Russia.

TOP: **This well-camouflaged PzKpfw III has the long-barrelled 5cm/1.97in KwK39 L/60 gun fitted, unusually with a false muzzle brake.** ABOVE: **A column of PzKpfw III Ausf Js move through a Russian village. Over 1,500 of this model were produced between March 1941 and July 1942.** BELOW: **One way of getting a larger-calibre gun on to an existing tank chassis was via the *Sturmgescheutz* (assault gun/tank destroyer). This model mounted a 7.5cm/2.95in gun.**

PzKpfw III Ausf F Medium Tank

Entered service: 1937

Crew: 5

Weight: 19,500kg/19.2 tons

Dimensions: Length – 5.38m/17ft 8in
Height (over turret hatch) – 2.45m/8ft 0.5in
Width – 2.91m/9ft 7in

Armament: Main – 3.7cm/1.46in KwK gun (early models)
Secondary – 2 x 7.92mm/0.312in machine-guns

Armour: Maximum – 30mm/1.18in

Powerplant: Maybach HL120 TRM, V12 petrol, 223.7kW/300hp

Performance: Speed – 40kph/24.9mph
Range – 165km/102.5 miles

PzKpfw IV Medium Tank

Undoubtedly the best German medium tank was the PzKpfw IV, and it was the only German battle tank to remain in production throughout World War II, being constantly up-armoured and up-gunned. The PzKpfw IV was a well-made robust tank with a satisfactory cross-country performance and a large turret ring that enabled it to take more powerful guns.

The early models mounted a 7.5cm/2.95in L/24 low-velocity, short-barrelled gun in its role as an infantry support tank. Versions Ausf A–E had increased armour and therefore increased weight and the hull machine-gun, omitted on both the Ausf B and C, was again fitted from the Ausf D onwards.

In 1941 plans were laid to improve the firepower of PzKpfw IV by fitting a long-barrelled 7.5cm/2.95in gun. The Ausf F was the first to be so fitted, and stowage arrangements had to be modified to accept the larger rounds. When it first appeared in mid-1942, it was more than a match for any of the contemporary Allied tanks

The Ausf G was very like the Ausf F, with minor variations, including thicker side armour. More of the Ausf H was produced than any other model and had better transmission, thicker armour and a new idler. It was the penultimate model in the PzKpfw IV range.

Last of the line was the Ausf J, which weighed 25,401kg/25 tons, had a range of over 300km/186 miles and a top speed of 38kph/23.6mph. It was also fitted with *Schürzen* (skirts) to

TOP: **The Tank Museum's PzKpfw IV which, together with the PzKpfw III, was the backbone of the** *Panzerwaffe*, **remaining in quantity production from 1937 to 1945.** ABOVE: **A striking photograph of a PzKpfw IV Ausf C that appeared in** *SIGNAL*, **the German propaganda magazine.**

protect against HEAT (High-Explosive Anti-Tank) weapons and had extra "stand-off" armour around the turret. Its long-barrelled 7.5cm/2.95in gun had an excellent performance against enemy armour.

LEFT: **Early model PzKpfw IVs break through a wall into woodland during training prior to the invasion of the Low Countries in 1940.** BELOW LEFT: **A column of PzKpfw IV Ausf Hs make their way up to the Orel battle front in August 1943. Note the add-on "stand-off" armour around the turret to guard against bazooka-type weapons (also side plates to similarly protect the suspension).** BELOW: **These GIs of 35th US Infantry Division make their way carefully in this ruined town, skirting a knocked-out and abandoned PzKpfw IV.** BOTTOM: **An early model PzKpfw IV armed with the short-barrelled support 7.5cm/ 2.95in KwK37 L/24 gun waits to engage an enemy strongpoint while a Russian soldier crawls to safety – but was it staged for propaganda purposes?**

Like the PzKpfw III, the IV also had many variants in addition to the more obvious ones. There was a range of assault gun/ tank destroyers, including StuG IV, Jagdpanzer IV, Panzer IV 70(V) and Panzer IV 70(A), on up to *Hornisse* which mounted an 8.8cm/3.46in anti-tank gun. Then there was a range of AA guns (*Flakpanzer*) and numerous self-propelled howitzers and various types of bridges. However, probably the most unusual was the ammunition carrier for the SP heavy siege mortar *Karlgerät* that could carry four of its massive 60cm/23.61in rounds in specially designed racks above the engine compartment!

PzKpfw IV Ausf F2 Medium Tank

Entered service: 1942
Crew: 5
Weight: 22,350kg/22 tons
Dimensions: Length – 6.63m/21ft 9in
  Height (over turret hatch) – 2.68m/8ft 9.5in
  Width – 2.88m/9ft 5.5in
Armament: Main – 7.5cm/2.95in KwK40 L/43 gun
  Secondary – 2 x 7.92mm/0.312in machine-guns
Armour: Maximum – 50mm/1.97in
Powerplant: Maybach HL120 TRIM, V12 petrol, 223.7kW/300hp
Performance: Speed – 40kph/24.9mph
  Range – 209km/129.9 miles

PzKpfw V Panther Heavy Tank

As World War II progressed, the Germans maintained their tank superiority by bringing the PzKpfw V and VI heavy tanks into service in the 40,640–60,960kg/40–60 ton range, well ahead of the Allies. PzKpfw V, or Panther as it is more commonly known, owes much of its design to a detailed study undertaken of the Russian T-34 which had proved to be greatly superior to the PzKpfw III and IV. The Ausf D model Panther, appearing in 1943, weighed 43,690kg/43 tons, mounted a 7.5cm/2.95in KwK42 L/70 gun and had a crew

of five. With a top speed of about 45kph/28mph, and a radius of action of 200km/124.3 miles, it was a formidable opponent.

A total of 850 of the Ausf D model were built, and it was the first to go into service despite the fact that the next model following it was called Ausf A! Some 2,000 Ausf As were built between August 1943 and May 1944. It had various improvements over its predecessor, including better running gear, thicker armour and a new commander's cupola.

The Ausf G was produced as a result of combat experience with the Ausf D

ABOVE: **This Panther is in the show ring at the French Armour School, Saumur – still in good running order.** BELOW: **A peasant family in their ancient horse-drawn cart pass a knocked-out Panther Ausf G in an Italian village.**

and A. Over 3,000 Ausf Gs were built between March 1944 and April 1945. The hull was redesigned, now without the driver's vision visor – which must have been a vulnerable spot. Variants included command and observation tanks and also the ARV (Armoured Recovery Vehicle) Bergepanther.

PzKpfw V Ausf G Heavy Tank

Entered service: 1944
Crew: 5
Weight: 45,465kg/45.5 tons
Dimensions: Length – 8.87m/29ft 1in
  Height (over turret hatch) – 2.97m/9ft 9in
  Width – 3.43m/11ft 3in
Armament: Main – 7.5cm/2.95in KwK42 L/70 gun
  Secondary – 2 x 7.92mm/0.312m machine-guns
Armour: Maximum – 100mm/3.94in
Powerplant: Maybach HL230P30 V12 petrol, 522kW/700hp
Performance: Speed – 46kph/28.75mph
  Range – 200km/125 miles

Jagdpanther Heavy Tank Destroyer

Of the various special adaptations of Panther, the Jagdpanther Heavy Tank Destroyer was perhaps the most famous. It mounted an 8.8cm/3.46in PaK43/3 L/71 gun which could penetrate 182mm/7.17in of armour at 500m/1,640ft. It was a well-protected, fast (46kph/ 28.6mph) and effective tank destroyer.

According to the official German handbook, the Jagdpanther was designed as a *Schwerpunkt* (literally "centre of gravity") weapon for the destruction of enemy tank attacks, and its employment as a complete battalion was considered to be the primary consideration towards achieving success. Production began in January 1944, and the first Jagdpanthers entered service in June 1944. Nearly 400 were built between January 1944 and March 1945. The Jagdpanther was undoubtedly the most important variant of the Panther.

ABOVE: **The Jagdpanther, sporting an unusual camouflage pattern. This tank destroyer mounted the fearsome 8.8cm/3.46in PaK43/3 L/71. Probably the largest concentration of Jagdpanthers was assembled for the Ardennes offensive in December 1944.** BELOW LEFT: **This abandoned Jagdpanther – note the unfired ammunition alongside the track – may well be badly damaged on the far side; certainly the idler wheel and track guard seem to have sustained a strike. 392 Jagdpanthers were built, the prototype being shown to Hitler in December 1943.**

Jagdpanther Heavy TD

Entered service: 1944
Crew: 5
Weight: 46,000kg/45.3 tons
Dimensions: Length – 9.9m/32ft 8in
  Height (over turret hatch) – 2.72m/8ft 11in
  Width – 3.42m/11ft 2.6in
Armament: Main – 8.8cm/3.46in anti-tank gun
  Secondary – 2 x 7.92mm/0.312m machine-guns
Armour: Maximum – 100mm/3.94in
Powerplant: Maybach HL230P30, V12 petrol,
  522kW/700hp
Performance: Speed – 46kph/28.6mph
  Range – 160km/99.4 miles

PzKpfw VI Ausf E Tiger 1 Heavy Tank

The most famous of all German World War II tanks was the Tiger, although only approximately 1,360 were ever produced – compared with 6,000 Panthers. Tiger production began in July 1942 and first saw action in Russia in August 1942.

Weighing 56,900kg/56 tons, the Tiger's main armament was the dreaded 8.8cm/3.46in KwK36 L/56 gun that could penetrate 110mm/4.33in of armour at 2,000m/6,561ft. To the average Allied soldier, the Tiger became the symbol of the invincibility of German armour – to a degree which completely outweighed its true capabilities – although when introduced, it was undoubtedly the world's most powerful tank. It did have weak points, however, one of them being its very low-gear turret traverse, which made bringing the main gun to bear on a target very slow.

ABOVE: **Probably the most famous tank of World War II was the German PzKpfw VI Ausf E, Tiger I. This was the first one ever captured complete by the British in North Africa, and is now in running order at the Tank Museum, Bovington.** BELOW: **Question: "When is a Tiger not a Tiger?" Answer: "When it has been specially made for the movies!". This excellent replica "Tiger I" was built using a T-34 chassis for the film *Saving Private Ryan*. It is seen here at a Bovington Tankfest in 2002. It is much smaller than the original but otherwise looks remarkably similar, apart from the running gear.**

PzKpfw VI Ausf E Tiger 1 Heavy Tank

Entered service: 1942
Crew: 5
Weight: 56,900kg/56 tons
Dimensions: Length – 8.45m/27ft 8.5in
    Height (over turret hatch) – 3m/9ft 10in
    Width – 3.56m/11ft 8in
Armament: Main – 8.8cm/3.46m KwK36 L/56 gun
    Secondary – 2 or 3 x 7.92mm/0.312in
    machine-guns
Armour: Maximum – 100mm/3.94in
Powerplant: Maybach HL210P45 V12 petrol,
    522kW/700hp
Performance: Speed – 37kph/22.9mph
    Range – 195km/121 miles

PzKpfw VI Ausf B Tiger 2 Heavy Tank

The *Königstiger* (Royal or King Tiger) or Tiger 2, as it was called, was a formidable tank that could deal with any of its opponents on the battlefield with ease. It weighed over 69,090kg/68 tons, was armed with a long-barrelled 8.8cm/3.46in KwK43 L/71 gun which could penetrate 132mm/5.19in of armour at 2,000m/6,561ft. It was thus able to deal effortlessly with the heaviest Allied tanks. However, its sheer weight and bulk gave it a relatively poor cross-country performance and made for problems in maintenance and reliability. Only 489 King Tigers were built, and they were used mainly in the defensive battles as the Allies advanced deep into Germany.

RIGHT: **This King Tiger has the much more streamlined Porsche turret, and is on show at the Tank Museum, Bovington. The King Tiger mounted the more powerful, longer-barrelled KwK43 L/71 8.8cm/3.46in gun.**

PzKpfw VI Jagdtiger Heavy Tank Destroyer

This monster tank destroyer, weighing 70,000kg/68.9 tons, mounted a 12.8cm/5.04in PaK44 L/55 gun and was undoubtedly the largest and most powerful armoured fighting vehicle to see combat service in World War II, its gun out-ranging most others. The 77 Jagdtigers that were built saw service in the Ardennes and later in the defence of the German "Fatherland".

PzKpfw VI Jagdtiger Heavy TD	
Entered service: 1944	
Crew: 6	
Weight: 70,000kg/68.9 tons	
Dimensions: Length – 10.65m/34ft 11.5in	
Height (over turret hatch) – 2.95m/9ft 8in	
Width – 3.63m/11ft 11in	
Armament: Main – 12.8cm/5.04in anti-tank gun	
Secondary – 2 x 7.92in/0.3in machine-guns	
Armour: Maximum – 250mm/9.8in	
Powerplant: Maybach HL230P30 V12 petrol, 522kW/700hp	
Performance: Speed – 38kph/23.6mph	
Range – 170km/105.6 miles	

LEFT: **Largest and heaviest of the Tiger conversions was the Jagdtiger, which mounted a massive 12.8cm/5.04in PaK44 L/55 gun that could penetrate 157mm/6.18in of armour at 1,500m/4,921ft. I once saw a Jagdtiger that had knocked out nearly an entire regiment of Shermans, but had then been knocked out itself by a *Jabo* (fighter-bomber).**

Renault FT-17 Light Tank and derivatives

Designed by Louis Renault, with the support of the irrepressible General Estienne, the Char Mitrailleuse Renault FT-17 was a remarkable little tank, a true milestone in design which lasted right up to the outbreak of World War II, and was adapted and produced by many countries all over the world. The American Ford 6 Ton Tank, for example, was in essence an American-built Renault FT.

A very large number of FT-17s were built, in seven different models, including a cast turret version. One unique aspect of the tank was its fully revolving turret – the first tank in the world to have all-round traverse. Armed with an 8mm/0.315mm Hotchkiss machine-gun, the two-man tank weighed just over 6 tons, was powered by a 26.1kW/35hp Renault engine and had vertical coil suspension. Later the Hotchkiss was replaced with a new 7.5mm/0.295in machine-gun.

The Renault factory received its first order for 150 F-17s in March 1917 and the first tanks appeared on the battlefield on May 31, 1918, at the Forest of Retz.

FT-17 in American Service

Renault FT-17 tanks were used by the US Army to equip the 344th and 345th Light Tank Battalions. Armed with a 37mm/1.46in gun in the turret and a machine-gun in the hull, they first saw action on September 12, 1918, under the command of Lieutenant Colonel George S. Patton, in an attack against the St Mihiel Salient, France.

TOP: **The most important French tank of World War I was the FT-17, and it was later copied by many other nations, including the Americans, Russians and Italians.** LEFT: **Armed with an 8mm/0.315in Hotchkiss machine-gun, the tiny 6,604kg/6.5-ton Char Mitrailleuse Renault FT-17, to give its full title, was the first tank in the world to have a fully traversing turret.**

FT-17 in Russian Service

Although the Russians now claim that they invented the tank, the first Russian tanks were actually 32 British Mark Vs and Medium Cs, plus 100 French Renault FT-17s, bought in 1918 by the Imperial Government, many of which were later captured by the Bolsheviks. They then acquired even more when the small British force withdrew from Russia and had to leave its tanks behind. The first Russian-built tank was a copy of the Renault FT-17, the KS (*KrasnoSormova*), after the place where it was built, but was also called the Russki-Renault. It would set the pattern for Soviet tank development over the next decade.

RIGHT: **A later post-war derivative of the FT-17 was this Soviet-designed and built MS-2 Light Tank, which had an entirely new sprung suspension and transverse engine. It mounted both a 37mm/1.46in gun and two machine-guns.**

ABOVE: **Another version of the ubiquitous little French tank had a moulded turret. FT-17s were still in service at the start of World War II, and some were still being used by the Vichy French in North Africa against Operation "Torch" (November 1942).** RIGHT: **An FT-17 in British Army service. The British used these small tanks for command and liaison work, normally (as here) with the gun removed.**

LEFT: **This version of the FT-17 mounted a 37mm/ 1.46in Puteaux gun. Some 1,830 of this model were built and, as can be seen, many are still in existence as monuments.**

Renault FT-17 Light Tank

Entered service: 1917
Crew: 2
Weight: 6,604kg/6.5 tons
Dimensions: Length – 4.09m/13ft 5in
  Height (over turret hatch) – 2.13m/7ft
  Width – 1.70m/5ft 7in
Armament: Main – 8mm/0.315in machine-gun or
  37mm/1.46 gun
Armour: Maximum – 22mm/0.87in
Powerplant: Renault 4-cylinder petrol, 26.1kW/35hp
Performance: Speed – 7.7kph/4.8mph
  Range – 35km/21.7 miles

Renault R-35 Light Tank

Following on from the disappointing AMC 34, Renault produced their AMC 35 model, which was very similar, but with a more powerful liquid-cooled 4-cylinder engine, an upgraded bell-crank scissors suspension system and improved vision devices. The hull was of riveted construction made with rolled steel plates. The turret armament remained the short-barrelled high-velocity 47mm/1.85in main gun, although some of the late models were fitted with a long-barrelled 25mm/0.98in Hotchkiss anti-tank gun and had a crew of three. The R-35 was the most numerous of the

French tanks to fight in 1940, but fared badly because it was found to have a high fuel consumption which limited its range. It was also out-gunned by the German AFVs.

ABOVE: **Most numerous of the French tanks to fight in May/June 1940 were the light infantry support Renault R-35, armed with a short-barrelled 37mm/1.46in gun. This one is taking part in the annual demonstration at the French Armour School, Saumur.** LEFT: **On parade in Paris pre-war, the Char Leger R-35, Renault Type ZM Light Tank had a crew of only two, so the commander also had to act as gunner traversing the turret by hand.** BELOW LEFT: **A file of R-35 light infantry support tanks on training. Some 2,000 were built, many of which were exported to Poland, Turkey and Romania. The Germans also used captured R-35s and gave some to Italy.**

Renault R-35 Light Tank
Entered service: 1935
Crew: 2 or 3
Weight: 14,500kg/14.3 tons
Dimensions: Length – 4.55m/14ft 11in
Height (over turret hatch) – 2.3m/7ft 6.5in
Width – 2.2m/7ft 2.5in
Armament: Main – 37mm/1.46in gun
Secondary – 7.5mm/0.295in machine-gun
Armour: Maximum – 45mm/1.77in
Powerplant: Renault, 4-cylinder petrol, 134.2kW/180hp
Performance: Speed – 42kph/26.1mph
Range – 160km/99.4 miles

Sentinel AC1, AC2, AC3 and AC4 Cruiser Tank

In late 1940, given the fragile state of supply between Britain and its colonies, it was decided to design a tank which could be produced in Australia, using easily obtainable items, such as truck engines. The Sentinel, as the result was called, was a tremendous achievement for a nation with such a small industrial base. It was initially produced in two versions, the first of these being the AC1, the most striking feature of this model being the very large sleeve for the bow machine-gun which was situated in the

centre of the hull. It also mounted a 2pdr main gun and had two Vickers machine-guns. The cast hull and turret were mounted on a suspension system which resembled the French Hotchkiss design, while various parts such as the final drives and transmission were copied from the American M3 Medium Tank.

Production began in 1942, and more than 60 tanks were built. However, these were only ever used for training. The second Sentinel model, the AC2, was not developed, so the next Sentinel to

reach the prototype stage was the AC3, which mounted a 25pdr howitzer in a larger turret. The triple engines (three Cadillac V8s) were now given a single crankcase. The AC3 did not progress further than testing. The next Sentinel model to be produced, the AC4, mounted a 17pdr, and this prototype was completed in 1943. However, with ample supplies of American tanks now being available, no further Sentinel production was required.

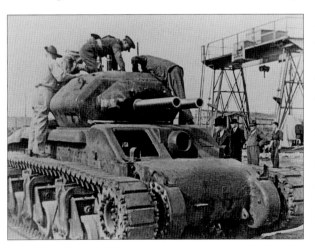

TOP: **A remarkable achievement for the infant Australian tank industry was the production of the Sentinel Cruiser Tank in 1942, seen here at the Tank Museum, Bovington. The AC1 was armed with a 2pdr gun.** LEFT: **Some prototype Sentinels were fitted with twin 25pdrs in order to simulate the recoil of an even larger weapon, like the 17pdr which was then tried in AC4 but never went into production.**

Sentinel AC1 Cruiser Tank

Entered service: 1942
Crew: 5
Weight: 28,489kg/28 tons
Dimensions: Length – 6.32m/20ft 9in
  Height (over turret hatch) – 2.57m/8ft 5in
  Width – 2.77m/9ft 1in
Armament: Main – 2pdr (40mm/1.58in) or
  25pdr (AC3) or 17pdr (AC4)
  Secondary – 2 x 7.62mm/0.3in machine-guns
Armour: Maximum – 65mm/2.56in
Powerplant: 3 x Cadillac V8 petrol, 87kW/117bhp
Performance: Speed – 48.3kph/30mph
  Range – 319km/198 miles

7TP Light Tank

In addition to the Carden-Loyds, another British export was the ubiquitous Vickers-Armstrong 6 Ton Mark E model, which was bought and copied by the Poles, who then in turn produced the 7TP – a 9,550kg/9.4-ton plus twin-turreted light tank with thicker armour than its progenitor. It was crewed by three men – the driver and one man in each turret, each armed with a 7.92mm/0.312in machine-gun (various models – Maxim, Browning and Hotchkiss – were tried). It was powered by a Polish-built Swiss-patterned Saurer 82kW/110hp 6-cylinder diesel engine.

The twin turrets of the first model were soon replaced by a single-turret variant, 7TP 2, still mounting a Bofors 37mm/1.46in gun. The final model, 7TP 3, came into production in 1937, with about 160 being built. It had thicker welded armour and now weighed 11,177kg/11 tons, a new engine and also a new turret produced in Sweden, which overhung to the rear, mounting the 37mm/1.46in Bofors high-velocity anti-tank gun, along with a coaxial 7.92mm/0.312in machine-gun. This was certainly the best tank the Poles had in service when the Germans invaded, with a few being modified and pressed into service by the Germans following their capture. Its Bofors gun was widely used by both sides in the war.

TOP: The Poles developed the British Vickers Armstrong 6 Ton Tank first as a twin-turreted model, but then as a single, mounting a 37mm/1.46in, which then went into production in 1937.

LEFT: The improved model of the 7TP Light Tank had better armour up to 40mm/1.58in thick and weighed 11,177kg/11 tons.

7TP Light Tank

Entered service: 1937
Crew: 3
Weight: 9,550kg/9.4 tons
Dimensions: Length – 4.6m/15ft 1in
    Height (over turret hatch) – 2.02m/6ft 7.5in
    Width – 2.16m/7ft 1in
Armament: Main – 37mm/1.46in anti-tank gun
    Secondary – 1 or 2 x 7.92mm/0.312in
    machine-guns
Armour: Maximum – 17mm/0.67in
Powerplant: Saurer 6-cylinder diesel, 82kW/110hp
Performance: Speed – 32kph/19.9mph
    Range – 160km/99.4 miles

SMK Heavy Tank

Two multi-turreted heavy tanks were designed by leading Soviet tank designer Kotin in 1938, each with three turrets, which were later reduced to two. They were designated as the T-100 and the SMK (the latter initials standing for Sergei Mironovich Kirov). They were almost identical in appearance, both having a an upper central turret mounting a 76.2mm/3in gun with all-round traverse and a lower front turret mounting a 45mm/1.77in gun which had 180-degree traverse only.

ABOVE AND BELOW: **The SMK (Sergei Mironovich Kirov) was another multi-turreted Soviet heavy tank that followed on after the T-35 and T-100. It closely resembled the T-100 and was used in the Russo-Finnish War, but proved to be lacking in both protection and firepower. It was abandoned in favour of the KV-1, which proved much more successful.**

The SMK, which at 45,722kg/45 tons was 11,177kg/11 tons lighter than the T-100, had a new torsion bar suspension, with eight independently sprung, smallish road wheels on either side

(with resilient rubber-bushed hubs) with four upper return rollers. The tracks were of a new design, with heavily spudded, small-pitch links. (Spuds are part of the metal track that juts out and provides traction.) The tank was constructed of cast armour, both on hull and turrets, that was designed to give protection against at least 37mm/1.46in anti-tank round at all ranges and was up to 60mm/2.36in thick.

A small number were used in Finland, but were not successful in combat, being difficult to manoeuvre and lacking both firepower and armour, so the project was abandoned in favour of the KV-1.

SMK Heavy Tank	
Entered service: 1939	
Crew: 7	
Weight: 45,722kg/45 tons	
Dimensions: Length – 9.66m/31ft 6in	
Height (over turret hatch) – 3.3m/10ft 10in	
Width – 3.45m/11ft 4in	
Armament: Main – 76.2mm/3in L11 and	
45mm/1.77in gun	
Secondary – 4 x 7.62mm/0.3in machine-guns	
Armour: Maximum – 60mm/2.36in	
Powerplant: AM-34 diesel	
Performance: Speed – 36kph/22.4mph	
Range – 150km/93.2 miles	

Skoda LT-35 Medium Tank

Developed in 1934 and in production the following year, the Skoda LT-35 was the main battle tank of the Czech Army during the years immediately preceding the German invasion, and was also sold to Romania. It had riveted armour, and its main 37mm/1.46in gun was developed from the Skoda anti-tank gun of the same calibre, renowned for its accuracy. There were also two 7.92mm/ 0.312in machine-guns, one mounted coaxially. Although generally reliable, it suffered from a few mechanical faults in its early life, which somewhat sullied its reputation. However, the proof of this vehicle's pedigree is that the Germans took over 200 into service, although they modified it and renamed it the PzKpfw 35(t).

They also continued to have it produced within Axis Europe until 1941, and it saw action in various theatres including Poland 1939, France 1940 and on the central Russian front up to 1941, where it reached the end of its front-line life and was thereafter relegated to secondary roles such as artillery tractor – *Artillerie Schlepper* 35(t).

BELOW: **The LT-35 in German service – now known as the PzKpfw 35(t).**

ABOVE: **This small Czech tank, the LT-35, was taken into service by the Germans and designated as the PzKpfw 35(t). Over 200 were acquired from the Czechs in March 1939. This model is at the Aberdeen Proving Ground in the USA.** LEFT: **The LT-35 was also in service with Romania and Slovakia pre-war, who purchased them in 1936–37 from the Czechs, as well as being in Czech service, as here.**

Skoda LT-35 Medium Tank

Entered service: 1935
Crew: 4
Weight: 10,670kg/10.5 tons
Dimensions: Length – 4.9m/16ft 1in
    Height (over turret hatch) – 2.21m/7ft 3in
    Width – 2.16m/7ft 1in
Armament: Main – 37mm/1.46in
    Secondary – 2 x 7.92mm/0.312in machine-guns
Armour: Maximum – 25mm/0.98in
Powerplant: Skoda T11 6-cylinder petrol, 89.5kW/120bhp
Performance: Speed – 35kph/22mph
    Range – 190km/118 miles

Skoda LT-38 Medium Tank

The Skoda LT-38 follows a similar history to that of the Skoda LT-35, although its quality was far superior to its predecessor, being reliable, hard-wearing and easy to maintain. Originally built for the export market by CKD, it was chosen by the Czech Army as the successor to the Skoda LT-35, with both companies co-producing the vehicle. The war then intervened, and the Germans were quick to pick up on the Skoda LT-38's value and pressed it into service for themselves.

By removing some of its ammunition and making room for a loader, they freed the vehicle's commander from that role and thereby still further improved the tank's overall performance. Later models had extra riveted armour, and following the vehicle's withdrawal from active service in 1942, the excellent chassis was used as the basis for both the Marder and Hetzer tank destroyers, as well as many others, one even mounting an 8.8cm/ 3.46in PaK43 (prototype only).

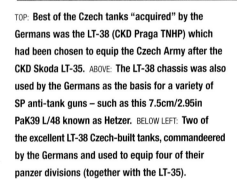

TOP: **Best of the Czech tanks "acquired" by the Germans was the LT-38 (CKD Praga TNHP) which had been chosen to equip the Czech Army after the CKD Skoda LT-35.** ABOVE: **The LT-38 chassis was also used by the Germans as the basis for a variety of SP anti-tank guns – such as this 7.5cm/2.95in PaK39 L/48 known as Hetzer.** BELOW LEFT: **Two of the excellent LT-38 Czech-built tanks, commandeered by the Germans and used to equip four of their panzer divisions (together with the LT-35).**

Skoda LT-38 Medium Tank

Entered service: 1938
Crew: 4
Weight: 9,400kg/9.25 tons
Dimensions: Length – 4.60m/15ft 1in
   Height (over turret hatch) – 2.4m/7ft 10in
   Width – 2.11m/6ft 11in
Armament: Main – 37mm/1.46in or 37mm/1.46in
   KwK L/40 or 37mm/1.46in L/45 gun
   Secondary – 2 x 7.92mm/0.312in machine-guns
Armour: Maximum – 25mm/0.98in
Powerplant: Praga EPA 16-cylinder petrol,
   93kW/125bhp
Performance: Speed – 42kph/26.1mph
   Range – 250km/155.3 miles

SOMUA S-35 Medium Tank

The SOMUA (its name an acronym of its producers: *Societe d'Outillage Mecanique d'Usinage d'Artillerie*) was the first tank with an all-cast construction of both hull and turret (which also had an electrically powered traverse), the thick armour providing excellent protection.

In the turret, the main armament was a long-barrelled high-velocity 47mm/ 1.85in gun, with a coaxial machine-gun alongside. The 141.7kW/190hp engine gave the S-35 a top speed of 40kph/ 25mph and a radius of action of 257km/ 160 miles. Fast and reliable, it was actually better armed and better armoured than its German opponents in 1940, but they were

not available in sufficient numbers, and, given the speed of the German attack, could not have made that much difference to the immediate outcome of events.

Some 500 of these 20-ton tanks were built and, like all contemporary French armour, were captured in large numbers

by the Germans and then pressed into their own service. As the tide of World War II turned, some came back once again into (Free) French hands, and they remained in service with the French Army for a considerable time after the end of the conflict.

ABOVE AND BELOW: **This French tank was probably one of the best medium tanks of the 1930s, with its 47mm/1.85in gun and 40mm/1.58in thick armour. This one belongs to the Bovington Tank Museum.**

ABOVE LEFT: **SOMUA S-35s like these fought in France in the 1940s, and captured models were used by both the Germans and Italians.**

SOMUA S-35 Medium Tank

Entered service: 1935
Crew: 3
Weight: 19,500kg/19.2 tons
Dimensions: Length – 5.38m/17ft 7.8in
    Height (over turret hatch) – 2.62m/8ft 7in
    Width – 2.12m/6ft 11.5in
Armament: Main – 47mm/1.85in gun
    Secondary – 7.5mm/0.295in machine-gun
Armour: Maximum – 40mm/1.58in
Powerplant: V8 petrol, 141.7kW/190hp
Performance: Speed – 40.7kph/25.3mph
    Range – 257km/160 miles

LEFT: Designed by the German tank designer Joseph Vollmer, who was responsible for the German LK I and LK II, the Swedish M/21 looked very similar to them. It had many new innovations, for example, the command version had a two-way radio, while the others just had receivers. In 1929 the engine was replaced with a more powerful Scania-Vabis.

Strv M/21 Light Tank	
Entered service: 1920	
Crew: 4	
Weight: 9,850kg/9.7 tons	
Dimensions: Length – 5.71m/18ft 9in	
Height (over turret hatch) – 2.51m/8ft 3in	
Width – 2.06m/6ft 9in	
Armament: Main – 6.5mm/0.256in machine-gun	
Armour: Maximum – 14mm/0.55in	
Powerplant: Daimler 4-cylinder petrol, 41.8kW/55hp	
Performance: Speed – 16kph/9.9mph	
Range – 150km/93.2miles	

Strv M/21 and M/29 Light Tanks

Despite the fact that Sweden has not taken part in any war since the beginning of the 20th century, they have still kept pace with the development of armoured fighting vehicles, having begun in 1921 with a copy of the German *Leichte Kampfwagen*. This is hardly surprising, as it was designed by Joseph Vollmer, the German engineer who designed and built the LK I and LK II and moved to Sweden after World War I. The Strv (*Stridsvagn* – "tank") M/21 was built in 1921 and was powered by a 4-cylinder 41.8kW/55hp Daimler engine. It had a crew of four and was armed with a single 6.5mm/0.256in machine-gun. The Strv M/29, produced in 1929, underwent a rebuild, having a more powerful Scania-Vabis 6-cylinder 59.7kW/80hp engine and heavier armour fitted, though the armament remained the same.

Strv M/31 Light Tank

By the late 1920s the Swedes had, with German assistance, established their own tank factory, the AB Landsverk Company at Landskrons. Their first design, which appeared in 1931, was a wheeled and tracked vehicle, with duplicate running gear. Two years later they produced the Strv M/31, which had a design that was well ahead of other nations, the turret and hull both being of welded construction.

The main armament of this four-man tank was a rapid-fire high-velocity 37mm/1.46in gun housed in a two-man turret with a coaxial machine-gun. The driver operated a second machine-gun.

It had a German Bussing V6 petrol engine, two-way radio communications, high-quality optical, sighting and vision devices.

Strv M/31 Light Tank	
Entered service: 1931	
Crew: 4	
Weight: 11,500kg/11.3 tons	
Dimensions: Length – 5.18m/17ft	
Height (over turret hatch) – 2.23m/7ft 4in	
Width – 2.13m/7ft	
Armament: Main – 37mm/1.46in gun	
Secondary – 2 x 6.5mm/0.256in machine-guns	
Armour: Maximum – 9mm/0.35in	
Powerplant: Bussing V6, petrol, 104.4kW/140hp	
Performance: Speed – 40kph/24.9mph	
Range – 200km/124.3 miles	

LEFT: Development continued with the AB Landsverk company producing a series of designs. This one, the Strv M/31 (L-10), was well ahead of its time. It weighed 11,500kg/11.3 tons, had a crew of four and mounted a 37mm/1.46in gun and two machine-guns.

Strv M/40, M/41 and M/42 Light Tanks

The Strvs of the early 1940s were another series of well designed light tanks from the Swedish AB Landsverk Company that can trace their ancestry back to the original Czech design. The Strv M/40 was the first to be produced in quantity. It was powered by a Scania-Vabis 105.9kW/142hp 6-cylinder engine, giving it a speed of just under 48.3kph/30mph, had a crew of three, and was armed with a 37mm/1.46in gun with two coaxial 8mm/0.315in machine-guns.

The Strv M/41, though similarly armed, had slightly thicker armour than its predecessor. To cope with the inevitable increase in weight, it was powered by an uprated Scania-Vabis 108kW/145hp engine.

The M/41 continued in service with the Swedish Army until the 1950s, when many were modified for use as armoured personnel carriers. The Strv M/42 was the first Swedish tank to mount a 75mm/2.95in main gun. Entering service in 1944, it weighed 22,353kg/22 tons and had a four-man crew. In the late 1950s the M/42 was rebuilt as the Strv 74, with a more powerful gun and thicker armour.

ABOVE: **Built to the basic design of the L/60 Light Tank, the M/40 L was the first Swedish tank to reach quantity production. This model is held at the Tank Museum, Bovington Camp.** LEFT: **The Strv M/42. This extremely modern-looking tank was designed by the Swedes in 1941–42. It was the first Swedish tank to be armed with a 75mm/2.95in gun. In 1958–60 it was modernized and rebuilt as the Strv 74.**

Strv M/41 Light Tank

Entered service: 1942
Crew: 3
Weight: 10,500kg/10.3 tons
Dimensions: Length – 4.57m/15ft
   Height (over turret hatch) – 2.37m/7ft 9in
   Width – 2.13m/7ft
Armament: Main – 37mm/1.46in gun
   Secondary – 2 x 6.5mm/0.256 machine-guns
Armour: Maximum – 25mm/0.98in
Powerplant: Scania-Vabis 6-cylinder petrol, 108kW/145hp
Performance: Speed – 45kph/28mph
   Range – 200km/124.3 miles

LEFT: **In the early 1920s the Americans built a number of prototype medium tanks – the M1921, the M1922 and the T1 of 1925. The latest model of the 1925 series was the T1E2, seen here, which had a crew of four and mounted a 57mm/2.24in gun. However, none of these models were put into production due to the demise of the Tank Corps and the upper weight limit of 15,240kg/ 15 tons being applied. The T1E2 weighed 22,352kg/22 tons and had a speed of 22.53kph/14mph, so it was well over the upper weight limit of 15,240kg/15 tons imposed by the War Department.**

T1 and T2 Medium Tanks

Three prototype medium tanks were built by the USA in the early 1920s: the Medium A of 1921; the Medium A2 of 1922; and the T1 of 1925. The main armament of the T1 was either a 57mm/ 2.24in gun or a 75mm/2.95in gun. It also had two 7.62mm/0.3in machine-guns.

Further development continued, with the next medium tank – designated the T2 – appearing in 1930. This had a semi-automatic 47mm/1.85in gun and a 12.7mm/0.5in machine-gun in the turret, plus a 37mm/1.46in and a 7.62mm/0.3in machine-gun in the right front of the hull. This dual mounting was later replaced by a single 7.62mm/ 0.3in machine-gun.

The T1 had weighed nearly 20 tons. The T2, however, had to conform to the new weight limit of 15 tons, as laid down by the US War Department. It weighed just 14 tons combat-loaded and was powered by a 252kW/338hp Liberty engine. The armament included a semi-automatic 57mm/2.24in main gun with a coaxial 12.7mm/0.5in Browning machine-gun plus two 7.62mm/0.3in machine-guns in sponsons. It had good cross-country performance and externally looked quite similar to the British Vickers Medium Mark II.

Three more prototypes were built – T3, T3E2 and T4 – all of which were based upon the designs of Walter Christie. They were all fast and reliable, but only lightly armoured, and none ever saw action.

T1 Medium Tank

Entered service: 1925
Crew: 4
Weight: 19,912kg/19.6 tons
Dimensions: Length – 6.55m/21ft 6in
  Height (over turret hatch) – 2.88m/9ft 5.5in
  Width – 2.44m/8ft
Armament: Main – Either 57mm/2.24in
  or 75mm/2.95in gun
  Secondary – 2 x 7.62mm/0.3in machine-guns
Armour: Maximum – 9.5mm/0.37in
Powerplant: Liberty V12 petrol, 252kW/338hp
Performance: Speed – 22.5kph/14mph
  Range – 56km/35 miles

ABOVE: **Next in line was the T2 Medium Tank, which bore a strong resemblance to the British Vickers Medium. It weighed only 14,225kg/14 tons, having been deliberately designed to conform with the US War Department's 15,240kg/15-ton weight limit.**

T-34/76A Medium Tank

One of the most unpleasant surprises experienced by the Germans in Russia came some five months after the launching of Operation "Barbarossa" in the shape of a new tank which inflicted heavy losses upon the PzKpfw IIIs and IVs. General Guderian was so impressed with the new Russian tank that he thought the quickest way for the Germans to deal with the situation would be to copy it! It was, of course, the T-34, one of the most important single elements in the eventual Russian victory.

Using a Christie-type suspension and mounting a 76.2mm/3in gun, the 31,390kg/30.9-ton tank had a crew of four and a top speed of 40kph/25mph. Well-armoured, robust and devoid of any frills, it was easily mass-produced – another vital factor in its favour. The next in the series, the T-34/76D, had a new hexagonal turret, with no overhang as on the previous models. This did away with the "bullet trap" which the overhang had created, and also made it more difficult for enemy soldiers who had climbed on to

the back to wedge Teller mines under the rear of the turret overhang. The T-34/76 was a critical tank at a critical time, and it helped the USSR stem and then turn the tide of World War II in their favour.

ABOVE: **Undoubtedly one of the best tanks of World War II was the Soviet T-34/76 Medium Tank, based upon the earlier T-32. It became the main Russian medium tank of the war.** BELOW LEFT: **These T-34/76Ds are advancing through the forests of Byelorussia. Note the entirely new hexagonal turret on this much improved production model.**

T-34/76A Medium Tank

Entered service: 1940
Crew: 4
Weight: 31,390kg/30.9 tons
Dimensions: Length – 6.09m/20ft
　　　　Height (over turret hatch) – 2.57m/8ft 5in
　　　　Width – 2.88m/9ft 5.5in
Armament: Main – 76.2mm/3in L41 gun
　　　　Secondary – 2 x 7.62mm/0.3in machine-guns
Armour: Maximum – 65mm/2.56in
Powerplant: V234 V12 diesel, developing 373kW/500hp
Performance: Speed – 40kph/25mph
　　　　Range – 430km/267.2 miles

T–34/85 Medium Tank

Towards the end of 1943 the T-34 was made even more lethal by the fitting of a new 85mm/3.35in gun in an enlarged turret. The new gun had an effective range of 1,000m/3,281ft and could penetrate the frontal armour of both the Tiger and Panther at that range – or so the Russians claimed. The German MBTs probably had the edge over their Soviet counterparts, but in the end the Russian tanks were available in far larger numbers, and this would be the decisive factor – quantity to overwhelm all opposition.

ABOVE: The T-34/85 was a much-improved model, giving it better firepower so as to match later German tanks. This one was photographed at Bovington. ABOVE RIGHT: The up-gunned version of the T-34 mounted the 85mm/3.35in gun in an enlarged turret. It is seen here at the Aberdeen Proving Ground in the USA.

BELOW LEFT AND RIGHT: Internal views of the T-34/85 at the Tank Museum. The first shows the driver's seat, instruments and one of his steering levers. The other shows the breech end of the main armament.

T-34/85 Medium Tank

Entered service: 1944
Crew: 5
Weight: 32,000kg/31.5 tons
Dimensions: Length – 8.15m/26ft 9in
　　Height (over turret hatch) – 2.74m/9ft
　　Width – 2.99m/9ft 9.5in
Armament: Main – 85mm/3.35in ZiS S53 gun
　　Secondary – 2 x 7.62mm/0.3in machine-guns
Armour: Maximum – 90mm/3.54in
Powerplant: V234 12-cylinder diesel, 373kW/500hp
Performance: Speed – 55kph/34.2mph
　　Range – 300km/186.4 miles

Turan I and II Medium Tanks

The first tanks in Hungary were Italian CV33 tankette imports in the 1930s. When World War II broke out, the government then attempted to purchase tanks from Czechoslovakia, but with their total production taken up by Germany, the Czechs could not oblige. Instead, Hungary obtained the rights to one of the latest Skoda tanks – the T-21 – which it then modified to suit its own military and industrial requirements. Powered by a Hungarian 8-cylinder 194kW/260hp

engine, equipped with leaf spring suspension and with the original two-man turret replaced with a three-man version equipped with radio communications, the Turan I mounted a Skoda 40mm/1.58in main gun and two 8mm/0.315in machine-guns – one of them coaxial and one in the hull – and had a crew of five. The Turan II had an upgraded 75mm/2.95in main gun mounted in a modified turret, but was otherwise the same as its predecessor.

ABOVE: **The Turan I Medium Tank was a 16,257kg/ 16-ton tank built under licence in Hungary and based on a Czech design.** BELOW: **Another Hungarian Turan Medium Tank, this time a Mark II, negotiates an ad hoc wooden bridge. The Mark II mounted a 75mm/2.95in gun instead of the original 40mm/ 1.58in.** BELOW LEFT: **This Turan Mark II has plenty of passengers. Its place in the Hungarian Armoured Corps was taken by German PzKpfw III and PzKpfw IVs.**

Turan II Medium Tank

Entered service: 1943
Crew: 5
Weight: 18,500kg/18.2 tons
Dimensions: Length – 5.69m/18ft 8in
    Height (over turret hatch) – 2.33m/7ft 7.5in
    Width – 2.54m/8ft 4in
Armament: Main – 75mm/2.95in gun
    Secondary – 2 x 8mm/0.315in machine-guns
Armour: Maximum – 50mm/1.97in
Powerplant: Weiss V8 petrol, 194kW/260hp
Performance: Speed – 47kph/29.2mph
    Range – 165km/102.5 miles

Type 3 Ka-Chi Amphibious Tank

The Japanese had long been interested in amphibious armoured vehicles for use by their Imperial Navy. Based upon the Chi-He design, the Ka-Chi was of an all-welded construction and had two detachable floats, one at the bow and one at the stern, that gave the tank its buoyancy while in the water and once ashore could be discarded. It was driven through the water by means of two propellers working off the main engine, while the commander steered via twin rudders which he operated from his turret. Powered by a 179kW/240hp V12 diesel engine and operated by a crew of seven, the Ka-Chi mounted a 47mm/1.85in main gun along with two 7.7mm/0.303in machine-guns – one of them mounted coaxially in a turret which was surmounted by a cylindrical chimney, providing an escape hatch for the crew.

Type 3 Ka-Chi Amphibious Tank	
Entered service: 1942	
Crew: 7	
Weight: 28,700kg/28.3 tons	
Dimensions: Length – 10.3m/33ft 9.5in	
Height (over turret hatch) – 3.82m/12ft 6.5in	
Width – 3m/9ft 10in	
Armament: Main – 47mm/1.85in gun	
Secondary – 2 x 7.7mm/0.303in machine-guns	
Armour: Maximum – 50mm/1.97in	
Powerplant: Mitsubishi 100 V12 diesel, 179kW/240hp	
Performance: Speed – 32kph/19.9mph	
Range – 319km/198.2 miles	

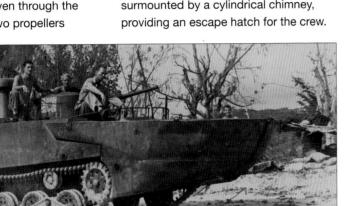

LEFT: **The Type 3 Ka-Chi Amphibious Tank, seen here out of the water after its capture by the Americans. Weighing 28,700kg/28.3 tons, mainly due to its large, detachable pontoons, it was developed by the Japanese Navy after the Army lost interest in amphibians. Note the submarine-type escape hatch on the top of the turret.**

Type 5 To-Ku Amphibious Tank

Largest of the Japanese amphibious tanks was the Type 5 To-Ku, the increase in size enabling an increase in firepower. It mounted a 47mm/1.85in main gun and a machine-gun in the front of its hull with a further 25mm/0.98in naval cannon and a coaxial machine-gun in its turret. However, the vehicle never reached full production before the end of World War II.

Type 5 To-Ku Amphibious Tank	
Entered service: 1945	
Crew: 7	
Weight: 29,465kgkg/29 tons	
Dimensions: Length – 10.81m/35ft 5.5in	
Height (over turret hatch) – 3.00m/9ft 10in	
Width – 3.38m/11ft 1 in	
Armament: Main – 47mm/1.85in gun and 25mm/0.98in cannon	
Secondary – 2 x 7.7mm/0.303in machine-guns	
Armour: Maximum – 50mm/1.97in	
Powerplant: Type 100 V12 diesel, 179kW/240hp	
Performance: Speed – 32kph/20mph	
Range – 319km/198 miles	

LEFT: **The Type 5 To-Ku Amphibious Tank was the largest of the Japanese amphibious tanks and mounted a 47mm/1.85in gun and a machine-gun in its front hull, while in the turret was a naval 25mm/0.98in cannon and another machine-gun. It weighed 29,465kg/29 tons with its pontoons. On this model the escape tower had been done away with.**

Type 95 Ha-Go Light Tank

Speedy and reliable, the Ha-Go was one of the best tanks to be built by the Japanese, and it saw action in China and then throughout the Far East in World War II. It was powered by an advanced 6-cylinder 89.5kW/120hp diesel engine giving it a speed of 45kph/28mph, steered by the clutch and brake method with front drive sprockets and had a sliding transmission allowing four forward and one reverse gear. Its small turret was offset to the left and mounted a 37mm/1.46in gun as its main armament, with another coaxial 7.7mm/0.303in machine-gun alongside. The somewhat bulbous superstructure protruded out over the tracks with an extra prominence for the bow 7.7mm/0.303in machine-gun.

The tank had a crew of three and suffered from the disadvantage of having the bow machine-gunner seated next to the driver in the hull leaving the commander to load, aim and fire the

ABOVE LEFT: **Undoubtedly the most-used small Japanese tank of the war. The Type 95 Ha-Go saw action in China and then throughout the Far East.**
ABOVE: **An excellent photograph of a Japanese tank commander standing proudly in front of his three-man Ha-Go.** BELOW LEFT: **The main armament of the Ha-Go was a 37mm/1.46in gun, and it also had two machine-guns. With a crew of three, it had a top speed of 45kph/28mph.**

turret guns by himself. There was also an amphibious version based on the Ha-Go that was known as the Type 2 Ka-Mi and intended for Japanese Navy use. Some 1,350 Ha-Go were built between 1935–43.

Type 95 Ha-Go Light Tank
Entered service: 1935
Crew: 3
Weight: 7,400kg/7.28 tons
Dimensions: Length – 4.38m/14ft 4.5in   Height (over turret hatch) – 2.18m/7ft 2in   Width – 2.06m/6ft 9in
Armament: Main – 37mm/1.46in gun   Secondary – 2 x 7.7mm/0.303in machine-guns
Armour: Maximum – 12mm/0.47in
Powerplant: Mitsubishi NVD 6-cylinder diesel, 89.5kW/120hp
Performance: Speed – 45kph/28mph   Range – 242km/150.4 miles

LEFT: **The Type 89 Ot-Su Medium Tank was developed from the British Vickers Medium. Its main armament was a 57mm/2.24in gun.**

Type 89B Ot-Su Medium Tank	

Entered service: 1936 (designed in 1929)
Crew: 4
Weight: 13,000kg/12.8 tons
Dimensions: Length – 5.73m/18ft 9.5in
    Height (over turret hatch) – 2.56m/8ft 5in
    Width – 2.13m/7ft
Armament: Main – 57mm/2.24in gun
    Secondary – 2 x 6.5mm/0.256in machine-guns
Armour: Maximum – 17mm/0.67in
Powerplant: Mitsubishi 6-cylinder diesel, 89.5kW/120hp
Performance: Speed – 26kph/16.2mph
    Range – 170km/105.6 miles

Type 89B Ot-Su Medium Tank

Having obtained a Vickers Medium C from Britain, the Japanese Osaka Arsenal produced a modified version in the Type 89 Light Tank of just under 10,160kg/10 tons, mounting a 57mm/2.24in main gun and two machine-guns. They were so delighted with this design that they used it as the basis for a heavier medium tank (Type 89) which was standardized in 1929. From 1936, a diesel version of this tank, the Type 89B, was developed by Mitsubishi and remained in service during most of World War II.

There were two versions; the first had a one-piece front plate, the driver being located on the left. Main armament was a Type 90 57mm/2.24in gun and there was a 6.5mm/0.256in machine-gun at the rear of the turret, plus another one on the right of the front plate. The second model had the driver's position and machine-gun reversed, while the front plate was all in one piece. The skirting plates had also been redesigned, with four return rollers in place of the five girder-mounted return rollers of the previous model, while the armament remained the same.

Like most Japanese tanks, the Ot-Su fared badly against Allied armour such as the M4 Sherman because they were undergunned and underarmoured by comparison, due to the Japanese disinterest in tanks for most of the war.

Type 97 Chi-Ha Medium Tank

Probably the most successful of all Japanese tank designs, the Chi-Ha saw service throughout World War II, having been selected for mass production in 1937. However, its medium status could really only be considered in Japanese tank production, for in combat it was no match for the Sherman or other Allied medium tanks. It was essentially a scaled-up version of the Type 95 Ha-Go Light Tank fitted with a two-man turret and armed with a 57mm/2.24in short-barrelled main gun and two machine-guns, one of which was mounted at the turret rear. With a crew of four, this tank weighed nearly 15 tons, had a helical suspension system with clutch and brake steering, and was powered by a 126.8kW/170hp air-cooled diesel engine with a top speed of 39kph/24mph. As the war progressed and the Japanese came to realize just how underdeveloped their AFVs were when compared with the opposition, the demand grew for more powerful equipment. A later development (1942) was the Shinhoto Chi-Ha ("New Turret" Chi-Ha), an interim model Type 97 Chi-Ha fitted with a modified turret which mounted a long-barrelled, high-velocity 47mm/1.85in main gun.

Type 97 Chi-Ha Medium Tank	

Entered service: 1937
Crew: 4
Weight: 15,000kg/14.8 tons
Dimensions: Length – 5.5m/18ft 0.5in
    Height (over turret hatch) – 2.23m/7ft 4in
    Width – 2.33m/7ft 7.5in
Armament: Main – 57mm/2.24in gun
    Secondary – 2 x 7.7mm/0.303 machine-guns
Armour: Maximum – 25mm/0.98in
Powerplant: Mitsubishi 97 V12 diesel, 126.8kW/170hp
Performance: Speed – 39kph/24.2mph
    Range – 200km/124.3 miles

LEFT: **This Chi-Ha was photographed at the Aberdeen Proving Ground in the USA. Unfortunately, most of their exhibits are outdoors, so they inevitably deteriorate.**

Vickers Commercial Dutchman Light Tank

ABOVE: **A modern photograph of the Bovington Tank Museum's "Dutchman" in its striking pre-war camouflage. Mechanically similar to the Vickers Mark IV Light Tank, it was powered by a Meadows 65.6kW/88bhp engine.**

Between the wars, Vickers Armstrong, having absorbed Carden-Loyd, became a major player in the international arms industry, building prototypes and exporting AFVs all over the world. The Commercial Dutchman was one such venture, sold to the Dutch East Indies and China. Some were still in the UK when war broke out and were pressed into service, although used only for training. This vehicle was to all intents and purposes mechanically the same as the Vickers Light Mark IV, the only major difference being its hexagonally shaped turret.

BELOW: **Sharing this colourful stand with the Vickers 6 Ton at the Bovington Tank Museum is the other Vickers export model, the Light Tank, Model 1936, also known as the "Dutchman" (it was sold to China and to the Dutch East Indies).**

Vickers Commercial Dutchman Light Tank

Entered service: 1936
Crew: 2
Weight: 3,860kg/3.8 tons
Dimensions: Length – 3.63m/11ft 11in
  Height (over turret hatch) – 2m/6ft 7in
  Width – 1.8m/5ft 11in
Armament: Main – Vickers 7.7mm/0.303in MG
Armour: Maximum – 10mm/0.39in
Powerplant: Meadows 6-cylinder, 65.6kW/88bhp
Performance: Speed – 65kph/40mph
  Range – 209.2km/130 miles

Vickers 6 Ton Tank

Although the British Army was not interested in purchasing the Vickers 6 Ton Tank, it became one of the bestsellers of its day – being exported to many countries, including the USSR, Poland, Bulgaria, Greece, Finland, Portugal, Bolivia, Thailand and China. The first versions had twin turrets with Vickers 7.7mm/0.303in machine-guns, and the later ones a 3pdr (47mm/1.85in) main gun and coaxial machine-gun in a single turret. The Vickers 6 Ton had a crew of three and featured some new features, including a "Laryngophone" system for internal communication, new improved suspension and had a fitted fireproof partition separating the engine from the fighting compartment. For some countries it was an influential design that

was copied (such as the Polish 7TP and Russian T-26), being mechanically straightforward and, for its size, well-armoured with good firepower.

Although rejected by the British, they established a formidable combat record in foreign service. For example, they saw action for the first time in the Gran Chaco War, when Bolivian 6 Tonners fought in the battle for Nanawa in August 1933. Later, in both the Spanish Civil War and the Winter War between Russia and Finland, 6 Tonners fought each other. It was also one of the principal tanks of the Polish armoured corps, so fought against the German invasion in 1939. The Chinese used theirs against the Japanese in Manchuria, and the Thais did the same in the 1940–41 war against Indo-China.

ABOVE: **Although it was called the Vickers 6 Ton Tank, it actually weighed 7,115kg/7 tons! It was sold (and copied) all over the world, but was not initially purchased by the British Army. They did eventually take over some of the undelivered overseas orders and used them for training purposes when World War II began in 1939.**

Vickers 6 Ton Tank	

Entered service: 1928
Crew: 3
Weight: 7,115kg/7 tons
Dimensions: Length – 4.57m/15ft
   Height (over turret hatch) – 2.08m/6ft 10in
   Width – 2.42m/7ft 11in
Armament: Main – 2 x 7.7mm/0.303in
   machine-guns (later, 1 x 3pdr and 1 machine-gun)
Armour: Maximum – 13mm/0.51in
Powerplant: Armstrong-Siddeley 4-cylinder petrol,
   64.8kW/87hp
Performance: Speed 32kph/20mph
   Range – 200km/124 miles

Glossary

"A" vehicle An armoured vehicle, wheeled or tracked.

AFV Armoured Fighting Vehicle – any armoured vehicle, whether tracked or wheeled, normally carrying an offensive weapon.

AP Armour-Piercing – ammunition that will penetrate armour plate rather than shatter or glance off on striking it.

APC Armoured Personnel Carrier – an AFV primarily designed to carry a number of fully equipped infantry soldiers.

ARV Armoured Recovery Vehicle – an AFV based on a tank chassis, crewed by fitters with the equipment to carry out the repair and recovery of most AFVs.

Ausf *Ausführung* (German) – the word used to differentiate between various batches or models of the same type of AFV.

automatic gun A weapon that loads, fires, extracts, ejects and reloads continually while the firing mechanism is engaged and the feed mechanism supplies ammunition.

"B" vehicle Any unarmoured vehicle normally wheeled. Also known as a "soft-skinned" vehicle.

calibre The diameter of the bore of a gun.

chassis That part of the tank that makes it mobile as opposed to the part for fighting.

coaxial The mounting of two weapons in the same mount.

cradle The non-recoiling part of the gun mount that allows elevation of the gun about the trunnions, houses the recoil system and guides it in recoil.

Cruiser Tank British term used to describe the series of lighter, faster, less well armoured tanks in between the lights and the mediums. Their role was to attack or counterattack with speed and panache, while the heavier infantry tanks supported the foot soldiers in the main assault. They would be absorbed into the medium range of tanks by the end of World War II. The term is now no longer used.

cupola A small protuberance above the main turret, equipped with vision devices and a protective lid, mainly for use by the tank commander.

CV *Carro Veloce* (Italian) – Fast Vehicle.

fascine A large bundle of pieces of wood (or nowadays metal pipes) carried on an AFV to be dropped into a ditch or hole to enable the tank to cross.

FV Fighting Vehicle, usually plus a number – British Defence Department nomenclature for British-built AFVs.

glacis plate The thick armour plate at the front of a tank, normally sloped at an angle so as to deflect enemy shot.

hatch An opening complete with cover and often vision devices, giving access in and out by crew members.

HE High-Explosive – the standard bursting explosive.

HEAT High-Explosive Anti-Tank – a type of projectile with a shaped charge that concentrates the explosion into a thin jet enabling it to penetrate armour plate.

Heavy Tank While the heavy tanks of World War I weighed only 28 tons, those of World War II were generally in the 50–60-ton bracket, or even heavier. Now they have been incorporated with the mediums under the general term MBT (Main Battle Tank).

idler The undriven guide wheel carrying the tank track.

Infantry Tank British term. These heavily armoured, relatively slow and, initially, cumbersome tanks were designed primarily to support dismounted infantry attacks, so speed was of little importance.

KwK *Kampfwagen Kanone* (German) – Tank Gun.

Light Tank In the past this term was used to describe small, fast, lightly armoured tanks in the 5–15-ton range, used mainly for reconnaissance, liaison and similar tasks. They were also ideal for training purposes because they were cheap and relatively easy to manufacture. In World War II their main reconnaissance role was taken over by armoured cars.

mantlet The moveable piece of armour plate that surrounds the hole into which the main armament is fitted into the turret. This hole has to be large enough to allow the gun to elevate and depress. It both protects and conceals this opening.

Medium Tank In the past this term was used to describe a tank of some 25–35 tons, reasonably well armoured and armed, with a good all-round performance. A perfect World War II example was the Russian T-34. Medium tanks have now been incorporated under the collective term of MBT (Main Battle Tank).

muzzle brake An attachment screwed on to the end of the gun barrel, deflecting the gases laterally so as to reduce recoil.

PAK *Panzer Abwehr Kanone* (German) – Anti-Tank Gun.

PzKpfw *Panzerkampfwagen* (German) – Tank.

rifling The spiral grooves in the bore of the gun that impart accuracy and stability to a projectile in flight.

roadwheel One of the wheels in contact with the track, which supports the tank.

semi-automatic gun A gun that requires the trigger to be pulled for each round fired.

skirting plates or side skirts Sheets of thin armour that hang in front of the upper run of the tracks and suspension. These cause HEAT projectiles to explode and thus dissipate their main force before reaching the hull.

sponson A projection mounting a weapon, located upon a tank hull.

sprocket A toothed wheel which engages with the track to drive it, and is itself driven by the engine.

suspension The wheels, tracks, rollers, roadwheels, bogies etc, on which the tank runs.

TD Tank Destroyer – a self-propelled anti-tank gun on a similar chassis to a tank but normally with lighter armour and an open top.

track The part of a tank that is in contact with the ground and is guided by the idler, sprocket and top rollers.

turret basket The floor attached to the rotating turret, so that the crew are rotated as the turret turns.

vision slot/slit An opening in the hull or turret through which a crew member can get a limited view outside.

Index

Acknowledgements

The author would like to thank the staff of the Tank Museum, Bovington, especially David Fletcher, Janice Tait and Roland Groom, for all their help.

The publisher would like to thank the following for the use of their pictures in the book (l=left, r=right, t=top, b=bottom, m=middle). Every effort has been made to acknowledge the pictures properly; however, we apologize if there are any unintentional omissions, which will be corrected in future editions.

Deutsche Panzermuseum Munster: 30t.

David Eshel: 10t.
George Forty: 20t; 20b; 21t; 21br; 22–3t; 24t; 24b; 26b; 27tr; 27b; 35br; 56m; 59t; 82tr; 82b; 112b; 113m; 118b; 122tr.
Richard P. Hunnicutt: 83tl (US Army).
Imperial War Museum: 38tr (TR 939).
Jim Osborne: 86b; 88b.
The Tank Museum, Bovington: 1; 2; 3; 4; 6t; 6b; 7l; 7r; 8–9; 10br; 11tl; 11tr; 11b; 12t; 12b; 13tl; 13tr; 13b; 14t; 14b; 15t; 15m; 15b; 16tl; 16tr; 16br; 17; 18t; 18b; 19tl; 19tr; 19b; 21bl; 22b; 23t; 23m; 23b; 24m; 25t; 25ml; 25mr; 25b; 26t; 27tl; 28–9; 30b; 31t; 31bl; 31br; 32t; 32b;

33t; 33b; 34t; 34b; 35t; 35bl; 36t; 36b; 37t; 37b; 38tl; 38b; 39t; 39b; 40; 41; 42t; 42b; 43t; 43b; 44t; 44b; 45t; 45bl; 45br; 46t; 46b; 47t; 47b; 48t; 49t; 49b; 50t; 50b; 51t; 51b; 52t; 52b; 53t; 53m; 53b; 54t; 55tl; 55tr; 55b; 56t; 56b; 57t; 57b; 58t; 58b; 60t; 60b; 61t; 61b; 62t; 62b; 63t; 63b; 64t; 64b; 65tl; 65tr; 65b; 66t; 66b; 67t; 67m; 67b; 68t; 68b; 69t; 69m; 69b; 70t; 70b; 71t; 71b; 72t; 72b; 73t; 73b; 74t; 74m; 74b; 75t; 75b; 76t; 76b; 77t; 77m; 77b; 78t; 78b; 79t; 79m; 79b; 80t; 80b; 81t; 81m; 81b; 82tl; 83tr; 83b; 84t; 84b; 85t; 85ml; 85mr; 85b; 86t; 87t; 88t; 90t; 90b; 93t; 93m; 93b;

94t; 94b; 95t; 95b; 96b; 97t; 97b; 98t; 98b; 99t; 99m; 99b; 120t; 100b; 101t; 101ml; 101b; 102t; 102b; 103t; 103b; 104t; 104b; 105t; 105b; 106t; 106b; 107t; 107ml; 107mr; 107b; 108t; 108m; 108b; 109t; 109b; 110t; 110b; 111t; 111b; 112tl; 113t; 113b; 114tl; 114tr; 114b; 115t; 115b; 116t; 116b; 117t; 117b; 119t; 119bl; 119br; 120t; 120m; 120b; 121t; 121b; 122tl; 122b; 123t; 124t; 124b; 125; 127; 128.

TRH Pictures: 48b; 54b; 59b; 89t; 89b; 91t; 91b; 92t; 92b; 96t; 112tr; 118t; 119m; 123b.
US Army: 87b; 101mr.
US Marine Corps: 87m.